BASEBALL'S GREATEST PITCHERS

by Milton J. Shapiro

photographs

Julian Messner
New York

Published simultaneously in the United States and Canada by
Julian Messner, a division of Simon & Schuster, Inc.,
1 West 39 Street, New York, N.Y. 10018. All rights reserved.

Copyright, ©, 1969 by Milton J. Shapiro

To my daughter, Sharon,
on her sixteenth birthday.

Printed in the United States of America
SBN 671-32093-9 Cloth Trade
671-32094-7 MCE
Library of Congress Catalog Card No. 69-13042

Contents

Introduction	7
Yesterday's Heroes	11
Whitey Ford	13
Sandy Koufax	42
Warren Spahn	65
Heroes of Today	81
Don Drysdale	83
Bob Gibson	105
Denny McLain	118
And Long, Long Ago	131
Grover Cleveland Alexander	133
Walter Johnson	143
Christy Mathewson	153
Cy Young	163
Records	175

Introduction

Who was the greatest pitcher who ever lived? The question has no answer, but can only solicit opinion. No one can name with certainty any pitcher at any moment in baseball history who was so superior in every facet of his position that he had no equal over his entire lifetime, and whose talent and accomplishments also transcended time.

Pitching yardsticks are too various, and the game has undergone too many changes to allow for such a man.

At least this is so for those great pitchers who now crowd the record books with their magnificent achievements. Perhaps someday there may emerge a man of such fantastic talent and durability that he will stand on top of the mountain by himself and be proclaimed all-time king of the pitchers. And even then, who knows but that he might be suspect? Perhaps such a man of the future will be a creation of science equipped with such talent and strength, out of all proportion to his fellow man, that he will be a superman of the mound.

The feats of such a man could not be fairly equated with the accomplishments of his predecessors. The author does not agree with those who say that a record is a record by itself. Since a record exists only in relation to the achievements surrounding and preceding it, then the circumstances, the rules of the game, and all pertinent background of the record-setting deed should be considered to provide fair comparison.

Thus, without reducing the magnificence of Roger Maris's 61 home runs, for example, the author feels that recognition should be made of the fact that it was accomplished in a 162-

game season. The record should stand alone, yes. But should not readers of the statistics be made aware that once upon a time, when the season was shorter, another record stood, and stood for many years?

Similarly, when a season might extend to 170 games, or 200 games, and a pitcher then wins 40 games, or someone hits 80 homers, should there not be note of the fact, when making up the new record books, that the rules had changed?

So it is with a comparison of pitchers from the beginnings of baseball to the present, and with the problem of choosing the greatest. So many variables have to be considered, in addition to the statistics. Just to name a few examples:

Earned-run averages, so meaningful, so indicative of a pitcher's talent, can be misleading. In the earlier days of baseball, and in fact almost up to World War II, relief pitching did not play nearly so important a part in the game. A pitcher remained in the game and took his lumps far beyond the point where, today, he would be replaced. Thus, many of today's pitchers enjoy lower earned-run averages because they are removed before greater damage can be done.

Again, this is not to denigrate in any way the record-setting ERA performance of Bob Gibson in 1968. His was a Hall of Fame performance, no question about it. The author repeats that these examples are given to indicate the difficulty in comparison of performances, either among pitchers who are contemporaries or among those who pitched in different eras.

Certainly strikeout records have to take into account the changes in the area of the strike zone. As this zone widens and narrows according to the decisions of the umpires and the general nature of baseball, so do a pitcher's chances for strikeouts change.

Think, too, of what night baseball has done. There are those who say it has helped pitchers, and those who say it has hurt. Certainly playing under the lights exerts some influence, and likely both for and against, depending upon the pitcher.

The same applies to the extension of the schedule, the

Introduction 9

expansion of the leagues, and the cross-country travel. All have effects upon hitter and pitcher alike, and must be taken into account when comparing the players of today and yesterday.

Another important point to be considered is the support given a pitcher by his team during his lifetime. Don Drysdale has one of the most remarkable records of poor support ever given any pitcher. Just a glance at his won-lost record would not tell anyone the true story of his worth as a pitcher and, indeed, would not merit him a place in this book.

For these and for numerous other reasons, there can be no agreement on the greatest pitcher who ever lived, nor indeed any agreement if one wanted to list the five all-time best. Even though Cy Young's 511 lifetime victories is a mark likely to stand forever (unless the schedule expands still further) there are those who contend that Christy Mathewson was a better pitcher.

The author is well aware that there will be those who will disagree with his choices for *Baseball's Greatest Pitchers*. In advance the author states that he agrees completely with the validity of all his critics' opinions. As long as they realize that it *is* opinion. In this book are presented the author's.

However, to lessen some of the inevitable outcry, homage is herewith paid to pitchers whose stories are not presented here, more due to the selectivity required by space, than to their standing in the author's estimation.

For the interest of the young reader of today, the author deliberately has given greater weight to modern pitchers. For this reason, and so that this volume would not assume the proportions of an encyclopedia, a number of truly great pitchers have not been included.

The author regrets the limitations that precluded chapters on such heroes of the mound as Carl Hubbell, Bob Feller, Satchel Paige, Early Wynn, Lefty Grove, Dizzy Dean and Juan Marichal.

Marichal in particular deserves mention, because his fine performance in 1968, when he won 26 and lost 9, was completely overshadowed by the record-breaking feats of Drysdale and Bob Gibson and Denny McLain's 31 victories. Their stories *are* presented here, therefore. But agreed, Marichal is one of the best in baseball today.

Certainly, however, the author will stand on this platform: his selections for *Baseball's Greatest Pitchers,* of this or any time, belong on anybody's list.

Finally, there are those few young hurlers, as yet incompletely tested by time, who deserve mention in light of recent achievement. There is Luis Tiant of the Indians, twenty-seven years old, who won 21 games in 1968 and led the league with a 1.60 ERA. Baltimore's Dave McNally, 22-10 in 1968, third in ERA with 1.95, is only twenty-five. Stan Bahnsen of the Yankees was 17-12 in his rookie season of 1968 and had a 2.06 ERA. Jim Hardin of Baltimore, who won 18, is only twenty-five.

In the National League, Jerry Koosman, 19-12, twenty-five years old, and Tom Seaver, 16-12, twenty-three years old, compiled those figures toiling for the Mets, giving added stature to their accomplishment. Koosman was also a rookie.

Someday, perhaps, these young stars will be included in a future volume about baseball's greatest pitchers. They have the look.

# Yesterday's Heroes ....

Whitey Ford

Whitey Ford

Eddie Ford was at loose ends. Here it was the autumn of 1945, the war had just ended, and suddenly he had no place to go. True, as a senior at New York's School of Aviation Trades he was learning to be a skilled aircraft mechanic—but with the war over, aircraft mechanics were a glut on the market.

Anyway, he had never really wanted to be an airplane mechanic; he had enrolled at SAT because his friend and sandlot teammate Johnny Martin had persuaded him to, mostly on the grounds that the school had one of the best baseball teams in the city.

So there he was, seventeen years old, with a trade he didn't want and nobody needed, a year of school yet to go, and not even the prospect of being drafted into a wartime service to inspire him.

What was he to do? In which direction should he travel? To what goal, what career? Indeed, what really interested him?

As these thoughts whirled through young Ed Ford's mind that autumn and winter of 1945, an idea began to take form. It seemed, at first, grandiose, beyond normal ambition, a boy's fanciful dream—until some undefined moment that winter when Eddie Ford made up his mind to convert a dream to reality.

With his father away in the Merchant Marine, Eddie had nobody at home with whom to discuss it, except his mother. At the dinner table one night he told her.

"Mom," he announced, "I think I'm gonna be a baseball player."

Mrs. Ford nodded her head patiently. "And what happened to the airplane mechanic?"

"There's no future in it anymore," Eddie said. "Besides, it's not for me. I wasn't cut out to be a mechanic."

"And for a baseball player you are?"

"I think so, Mom. At least I'm gonna give it a real try."

It was a fact, his mother knew well, that Eddie Ford was considered an excellent baseball player in the neighborhood. He was the best pitcher on the high school team and on the team he played with in the Kiwanis League, the Thirty-fourth Avenue Boys. But that wasn't professional baseball. Still, he was a smart boy, a good boy, and if he wanted to try to be a baseball player, he had her prayers and her blessings. She told him so.

"Thanks, Mom," he told her. "If I don't make it, I don't make it. But at least I can always say I gave it a try."

And give it a try he did the following spring. A senior at Aviation Trades, he knew it was his last big chance to display his talents to the major league scouts that visited the local high school games regularly. He was determined to be so good they would all have to sit up and take notice—and fight for him with the big bonuses they were beginning to hand out to youngsters in those first postwar talent-hunting days.

But—such is the delicate stuff that youngsters' dreams are made of. In the New York high school baseball season of 1946 Ed Ford did not shine above them all. In fact, he was not even the best pitcher on his own team. That spring, from seemingly nowhere, a young hurler named Vito Valentinetti stole his thunder and became the big winner for Aviation Trades.

Valentinetti was no flash-in-the-pan, to be sure. He

was genuinely good enough to go on to a fair career with the White Sox and the Cubs. However, at the time of his rise to amateur stardom, he was a nonentity, and to be humbled by Valentinetti was a terrible blow to Ed Ford's hopes.

Relegated to second-class status on the team, he nevertheless won all three games he pitched that spring. The rest of the season he played first base, since sandlot days his alternate position.

Staggered, but still determined, Eddie decided that if the scouts would not come to discover him, then he would go to the scouts and proclaim his talents.

In July, therefore, after graduation, knowing the Yankees were holding their annual sandlot tryouts, he turned up at Yankee Stadium—but with a first baseman's mitt. Having been eclipsed by Valentinetti that spring, he felt that perhaps first base was his forte, not the pitcher's mound. He did realize that his size was against him here; he was only about five feet seven and slight of build. But he was a good, if not powerful hitter, and it was in his mind at the time that if he was going to impress the Yankees at all, it would be as a first sacker.

He was wrong. At least, partly wrong. Paul Krichell, one of the greatest scouts who ever lived, was running the tryouts. Krichell was not overly enthusiastic about the way Eddie handled himself at first, or in the batter's box. But there was something about the kid—he didn't know what it was, just, well, *something,* that indefinable something a scout can sense about a young athlete that makes the difference between an ordinary scout and a great one like Krichell.

He called Eddie over for a chat. "You do anything besides play first?" he asked him.

"I pitch," Eddie replied.

Krichell nodded. "I thought so. Well, take my advice kid and forget about first base. Stick to pitching."

Krichell turned to leave, but Eddie was too determined, too close to desperation now to allow himself to be dismissed so lightly. He called Krichell back and demanded an explanation.

Krichell obliged him. "You're too small and you can't hit well enough to ever make it as a first baseman." Then that feeling, that hunch, hit the scout once again. He hesitated, then said, "Look, kid, warm up on the side for a while and I'll let you pitch to a few batters. See what you got."

A few minutes later, Krichell was treated to what the youngster had. He saw Eddie on the mound, working smoothly, with unusual poise for a high school pitcher, and with a big, easy curve. He liked what he saw. The kid had what scouts called "the look of a pro."

However, Krichell felt that the time was not yet ripe to take on this young pitcher. He felt that in a year, with a bit of weight and strength added, a bit more amateur, perhaps semipro experience, Ford might be ready. Before he dismissed him with a chat and a pat of encouragement, he said to him, "Kid, you got a good curve there, but it's always the same curve. You gotta learn to throw it different speeds, make it break differently. Otherwise the good hitters will figure you out in no time and murder you."

Then he spent a few minutes with the youngster showing him how to grip the ball and throw it to achieve those desirable ends.

Eddie went home a little sadder, a little wiser, but no less determined than before. If little else, he had at least gained a personal audience with the Yankees' chief scout,

and had received what he believed to be a genuine invitation to return for another look the following summer.
There was still this summer to live through, however. A summer of baseball pitching for the Thirty-fourth Avenue Boys. He could not let his teammates down. Conversely, he made up his mind to pitch his heart out for them, and use, if he could, the new tricks Paul Krichell had briefly outlined to him.
As for that Yankee scout, he dismissed Ed Ford from his thoughts, relegating him to that fantastic card-filing system he kept in the back of his mind. Someday, on an appropriate occasion, the card would pop up, all the data there, to remind the scout of what it was that had attracted him to that particular boy.
The appropriate occasion, for Ed Ford, came sooner than either of the two would have anticipated.
On September 28, two months after the Stadium tryouts, Krichell went to the Polo Grounds to watch the playoffs of the official sandlot championship of New York, sponsored by the New York *Journal American*. It was a game that attracted scouts from all the major league teams, for here could be seen the cream of amateur talent.
Until he arrived and looked at the lineups, Krichell had no idea that Ed Ford would be in there, pitching for his Kiwanis League champions. The youngster's record impressed him: 32–1, with a no-hitter included.
Soon enough he was even further impressed. He saw a young hurler who in two months' time had virtually mastered an entire repertoire of curves. Krichell was astounded. He watched, fascinated, as inning after inning Eddie spun his mound magic, throwing big curves and little curves, slow ones and fast ones, curves that arced like a rainbow and curves that snapped at the end like a whiplash.
Eddie had to be at his best that afternoon. The op-

posing pitcher, Lou DeAngelis of the Bay Ridge Cubs, was matching him inning for inning. At the end of ten scoreless frames, Eddie had given up two hits—but his mates had managed only one.

At the top of the eleventh Ed led off the hitting. He grabbed a bat and said to his friend and batterymate Johnny Martin, "This has gone far enough. I guess I'll have to win this one for myself."

Two pitches later he smacked the ball into left center field for a double. After an out and a hit batsman, another double scored him before DeAngelis retired the side.

Taking his 1–0 lead into the bottom half of the eleventh, Eddie drew on his last reserves of strength. His determination, his whole future rode on every pitch now. The ball became a dancing, tantalizing blur to the Cub hitters. Three men came up and three men struck out.

Eddie had his 1–0 victory, with 18 strikeouts in 11 innings.

For his performance in winning the New York City Sandlot Championship for his team, Ed was given the Lou Gehrig Award as outstanding player of the game.

Now the Ford phone began to ring. The Dodgers offered him a three-thousand-dollar bonus to sign. The Red Sox matched it. The Giants raised the price by a thousand.

Ed pondered the offers. His father, home now from his sea service, advised him to wait a few days. Ed was willing. In fact he was hoping the Yankees would make a reasonable offer; it was his favorite team, and he felt it would be a championship team for many years to come. He wanted very much to be a part of that picture.

Krichell, the scout, had come away from the game with the idea of signing the young pitcher. But he was still in the process of discussing Ford with the Yankee management while the other teams were plunging in, waving contracts.

When he did call, finally, he found Ford receptive, but businesslike. He said to Ed, "I saw you pitch at the Polo Grounds. You looked good."

"I owe you something for that," Ed responded. "In fifteen minutes you taught me more about throwing a curve than I learned in all the years put together."

Krichell chuckled. "You learn fast, too. Listen," he went on, "you get any offers?"

Eddie played it straight and told him.

"Okay," Krichell said. "I'll top the Giants. I'll go five thousand."

Eddie hesitated. He had heard, indeed read so much about big bonuses paid to young players—$25,000, $35,000, even more.

Krichell seemed to sense Eddie's thoughts. "Look, kid," he said. "I'll tell you the truth. Your size is costing you money. A little guy like you, you might not make it to the majors at all. You're a risk. But I tell you what. I think you got what it takes, and I'd like to see you with the Yankees. I'll make it seven thousand. How's that?"

Eddie sighed. "Hold on a minute," he said, "I want to talk to my father." Mr. Ford had been sitting nearby, waiting, and now, as his son relayed the Yankees' offer, he smiled and nodded assent.

Eddie turned back to the phone. "Mr. Krichell, you got me," he said.

At seven thousand dollars, he was a fantastic bargain, as the Yankees, and every other team, would shortly see.

The first thing Eddie Ford picked up in professional baseball was a nickname. Reporting to the Butler farm team, in the Middle Atlantic League, Ed walked into the clubhouse and was met by manager Lefty Gomez. The former Yankee pitching ace, a good-humored man, took a look at Ed's blond hair and greeted him with, "Hiya, Whitey." It was Whitey Ford thereafter.

Whitey was at Butler to learn from Gomez, but by midseason, when Ford had an 8–2 mark, the Butler skipper wrote a report to the Yankees' front office in New York.

"I've never seen a kid like this," wrote Gomez. "He throws his curves so easy, so natural. And he picks up things so fast by himself all I have to do is sit on the bench and watch him."

During that season, too, Fresco Thompson, director of the Dodgers' farm system, dropped by Butler to have a look at what the Dodgers let get away.

"Boy, did we pull a boner," he confided to a baseball reporter later. "That Ford kid's worth fifty thousand. Trouble is, we spend so much time trying to find a kid who can throw a ball through a brick wall we overlook qualifications that are harder to find. Ford's got the curve ball of a pro who's been in baseball ten years."

Whitey completed his first season of professional baseball with a 13–4 record and an earned-run average of 3.84. He improved on this the following year with Norfolk of the Piedmont League, compiling a 16–8 record and a 2.85 ERA. Once more he was advanced a league, to Binghamton, an Eastern League farm team managed by George "Twinkletoes" Selkirk, a Yankee outfield star before the war.

Selkirk liked the brash, eager young pitcher from the start. He admired Whitey's forthright confidence, which was tempered by the young man's knowledge that he had much yet to learn about the refinements of pitching, the bits of polish and professional lore that mark the difference between a good minor league hurler and a major league ace.

Selkirk was not a pitcher. But he knew everything there was to know about hitting, and hitters. Furthermore, he knew how to coach, knew how to mix encouragement with discipline to help push a promising young player up the ladder.

He allowed Whitey to sit at his side on the bench and badger him with questions, as a pitcher to a hitter. What did a major league hitter look for in a particular situation? How did a good hitter try to "read" a new pitcher, guess what sort of pitch was on the way?

Dozens and dozens of questions such as these filled Whitey's probing mind. Selkirk tried to answer them all. He sensed that sitting next to him on the bench was a kid who would in a few years be one of the great names of the Yankees.

On the mound Whitey was cementing that feeling with brilliant pitching performances. However, sprightly young man that he was, he didn't see himself as a Yankee in years to come. He saw himself as a Yankee now.

He said to Selkirk one night, after a 2–1, eleventh-inning victory, "I think I'm ready for the Yankees."

Selkirk laughed. "Patience," he said. "You'll just have to wait until the Yankees agree with you."

Whitey even had the temerity to phone Paul Krichell in New York to suggest the Yankees might need him at once. The fact was, they might have indeed benefited from his services. Under the first-year management of Casey Stengel, the Bronx Bombers were suffering from mound troubles. Still, the feeling was that Ford was at least another year away. Krichell told him so.

"Be patient," the scout said. "Your time will come."

"Patient, patient," Whitey muttered after hanging up the phone. "Everybody says be patient."

For the rest of his season at Binghamton he demonstrated that patience, and showed, too, that he was ready for better things. With 16 wins and 5 losses, he led the league with a 1.61 earned-run average, and tied for the lead in strikeouts, with 151.

He was promoted once more, to Kansas City in the American Association, just a notch below the major leagues.

When he reported to manager Joe Kuhel in the spring of 1950 he shook the skipper's hand and said to him, "Don't count on me for too much. I may not be around that long."

"Where you goin'?" asked Kuhel, eyes twinkling. He had heard about this self-assured little left-hander.

"I feel it in my bones," Whitey said. "The Yankees will be coming after me before this season's over."

Kuhel was amused, but skeptical. The Yankees had won the pennant the year before, and with Ed Lopat, Allie Reynolds, Tommy Byrne and Vic Raschi now as their top four, they didn't seem likely to need help in any hurry.

Before the 1950 season was two months old, however, Kuhel had a change of heart. Ford was 6–3, and the Yankees were in trouble. The Tigers led the league. The Yankees were second, but hard pressed by the Red Sox and Indians. Stengel needed help. Pitching help particularly.

This time the brash Whitey was silent. It was Kuhel himself who did the talking. He phoned the Yankees and told them that if they wanted pitching help, Ford was ready to step into a Yankee uniform.

A week later, on June 30, a telegram arrived in the

Kansas City clubhouse. Whitey was to report at once to Boston, where the Yankees were engaging the Red Sox.

Whitey didn't have time to feel nervous about pitching his first game. His first day in Yankee pinstripes he was thrown into the game in relief of Tommy Byrne. It was his misfortune that afternoon to be facing a red-hot Boston team, and the Red Sox hitters racked him up for five runs and seven hits in the five innings he worked. The loss went to starting pitcher Byrne, however.

A week later he was given his first starting assignment, against the Philadelphia Athletics. Opposing him was Bobby Shantz, ace of the Philadelphia staff.

For six innings he outpitched Shantz. He had a 3–1 win in his grasp. He had been pressing, however, in his major league starting debut, pushing too hard. Now the pace began to tell. Two singles, a triple and a double put the A's in front, 4–3, before he got Elmer Valo on a foul pop to end the rally.

His shoulders sagged when he walked off the mound; his head was bowed with disappointment. But when he reached the dugout Stengel said to him, "You did good, kid. I gotta take you out for a pinch hitter this inning, but you did good."

A ninth-inning rally pulled the game out for the Yankees, 5–4. But Whitey was still looking for his first major league victory.

That came, at last, on July 17, when he beat Billy Pierce and the White Sox, 4–3. He needed help from relief pitcher Tom Ferrick with two out and bases loaded in the eighth—but Ferrick came through to nail down his first win.

Stengel saw that he had a potential winner on his hands. Still, at this point, he could not insert the young pitcher into the regular rotation. The Yankee skipper felt

Whitey Ford

he had to win with his four experienced regulars. He did, however, spot Whitey steadily against the weaker second-division teams, giving him the work he needed to gain experience and confidence.

Whitey thrived on the diet. After the White Sox win he shut out the Browns, then three-hit the Senators, 3–1.

As the back-up pitcher for the Yankees' Big Four, Whitey proved to be a marvel. By the end of August he had won six straight without a loss.

Jim Turner, the pitching coach, didn't know what to make of him. "I can't teach him a thing," he told the sportswriters. "He sits there and watches and learns for himself. He's taught himself how to make his fast ball alive—watch how he moves it out there. And his curve! For a kid his age, with his experience—it's a miracle!"

In September another youngster joined the team. He, too, sat on the bench and watched and learned, though he didn't get to play. But he and Whitey became good friends, and their rookie status gave them a bond that was to last for many years to come, and help the Yankees to many championships. That was Mickey Mantle.

Now, in midmonth, the Yankees engaged in a last-ditch battle for the pennant. Still half a game behind the Tigers, they entered Detroit for a vital three-game series. Unless they could win two of the three and gain the lead, their pennant hopes were slim indeed.

They took the first contest, 7–5, but the Tigers evened the score, 9–7. That brought matters down to the final game. The Tigers picked ace Dizzy Trout to start. Stengel, of course, was expected to choose one of his veterans. Instead, he named Whitey to start.

The decision came as a shock to everybody, including Whitey himself. The sportswriters thought Stengel had chosen badly.

"The kid'll choke up," one writer said. "He's not used to this kind of pressure. He's been beating the patsies all year."

It was a grueling duel indeed. Whitey felt the tension, as fifty-six thousand Tiger partisans in Briggs Stadium roared with every pitch. For five innings he and Trout dueled scorelessly. Then, in the sixth, Joe DiMaggio homered for a 1–0 Yankee lead. Whitey held through the sixth and seventh, but doubles by Gerry Priddy and Vic Wertz tied the score in the eighth.

Inspired by their rookie hurler's game performance, the Yankees rose up in the ninth and broke the game wide open. Seven runs crossed the plate before the uprising was quelled.

Now it was Whitey's turn, in the bottom of the ninth, to exhibit similar inspiration—which he did by striking out the side!

The Yankees were in first place now, and they knew nothing could stop them. Whitey won two more games in the final-stretch run to the pennant, giving him nine straight victories. His bid for a perfect season was ruined in the season's final series against the A's, when he was beaten in the ninth inning by a home run.

His sensational 9–1 record and courageous victory over the Tigers won him a World Series assignment. After the Yankees took three straight against the Phillies, Stengel felt it was well worth the risk to give his rookie ace a chance to gain a World Series win, too.

Whitey proved once again he was no risk at all. While his mates were picking up five runs for him, he breezed through eight innings, scattering six hits, striking out six.

In the ninth inning, two men on base, two out—one out away from a World Series shutout, he got Andy

Whitey Ford

Seminick to loft an easy fly ball to left field. But Gene Woodling misjudged the ball, dropped it—and two runs crossed the plate.

A bit shaken, he allowed the next batter a single, and Stengel took him out. Allie Reynolds came on, struck out pinch-hitter Stan Lopata, and Whitey had his first World Series victory, the Yankees another World's Championship.

In the clubhouse celebration after the victory, manager Stengel was proclaiming long and loud for all to hear: "That Ford feller's the best rookie pitcher I've ever seen. He'll win a million before he's through up here!"

Whitey had been too young for World War II, but when the Korean conflict broke out, he was drafted into the Army Signal Corps. He wasn't shipped overseas, but served two years with a radar unit at Fort Monmouth, New Jersey.

When he returned to baseball in the spring of 1953 there was obvious doubt in Yankee minds about his condition. Two years away from professional baseball was a long time, especially for a pitcher. Too, he was overweight, and the muscles he used as a Signal Corps soldier had little in common with those needed by a major league pitcher.

Whitey found, too, that the Yankees had changed radically while he was away. Gone into retirement were Joe DiMaggio and Tommy Henrich, marking the end of the so-called Joe McCarthy era of the Yankees—those great powerhouses managed by "Marse Joe" before the war. Gone also were relief ace Joe Page, and Tommy Byrne, Jackie Jensen, Cliff Mapes, Johnny Hopp and Billy Johnson.

New faces were in the locker room. There was Mantle, already on the way to superstardom, and a youngster named Gil McDougald, and new pitchers named Tom Morgan and Bob Kuzava and Ray Scarborough.

Whitey worked like a beaver that spring of 1953. It was almost as though he had to prove himself all over again. He ran and he pitched and he chased fungoes in the outfield. He worked with veteran Ed Lopat on the league's new hitters, and with coach Turner on his control and his curve.

By opening day he felt he was ready. Stengel didn't agree. "You've been out of action two years," Casey said. "Let's crank up the arm in a relief spot once or twice to see how you do."

Whitey didn't like the decision. Still, Stengel was the skipper. All that could be done was to convince him, as soon as possible, that the two years had not taken their toll.

Whitey made up his mind to show him at first opportunity. Accordingly, a week after opening day, called into relief of Allie Reynolds in the sixth inning, he struck out the first two men he faced, then swept through the final three innings without a score against him.

"How about that, Skipper!" he said to Stengel in the clubhouse afterward. "Do I rate a start now, or don't I?"

"Yeah, yeah, quit your nagging," said Casey, winking across the room at coach Turner.

Again Stengel eased Whitey into competition by starting him against the second-division clubs. But, as soon as he felt that the youngster had gained his rhythm and his momentum, he put him in against the big clubs. Whitey repaid his skipper's confidence with an 11–1 victory over the Indians the first time he faced them. Then, two weeks later, he beat them again, 6–0, hurling a sensational one-hitter. Only an infield single by pitcher Early Wynn in the sixth inning spoiled his no-hitter.

After that victory Stengel gave him the No. 1 spot in the pitching rotation. "I wouldn't be afraid to use this little feller in the biggest game of the year," the Yankee pilot announced.

Whitey wasn't, in the literal sense, "little." He was five feet ten and weighed about 170 pounds. However, for a major league pitcher, he was undersized, the majority of the better ones coming in over six feet and weighing 200 or more.

With Whitey leading the way, the unbeatable Yankees roared to a fifth straight pennant, and then an unprecedented fifth straight World's Championship.

Whitey had bad luck in the World Series against the Dodgers. The Yankees were leading, two games to one, when he started the fourth game. A two-base error by Hank Bauer on leadoff batter Junior Gilliam's fly ball started the trouble. Then, when a double play would have ended the inning with just one run scoring, Jackie Robinson slid into second so hard he took Phil Rizzuto out of action, keeping the inning alive. A wild pitch and a double, and the score was 3–0.

Tom Gorman replaced Whitey, but the Dodgers went on to win, 7–3, tagging Ford with his first World Series defeat.

The Yankees won the next game, 11–7. Stengel, showing his confidence in Whitey, chose him to try for the final victory.

Pitching beautifully this time, he had a 3–1 lead in the seventh inning when he felt his elbow jerk with pain. He continued to throw, got through the inning, but the pain was terrible. Stengel saw something was amiss, saw

Whitey's face pale and drawn. He took him out of the game.

Reynolds, in relief, gave up two runs in the eighth. The score was tied. Whitey was no longer the pitcher of record. Thus, when the Yankees won in the ninth, credit for the victory went instead to Reynolds.

Despite the disappointment of the Series, the 1953 season was tremendously successful for Whitey. He had won 18, lost 6, and had established himself as the ace left-hander of the great New York Yankees.

It was a distinction that was to last for more than a decade.

After a bad start in 1954, Whitey won 15 of his final 20 starts for a record of 16–8. The Yankees' streak of five straight pennants was broken, however, by the Indians. What's more, it looked as though their hold on the league might be lost for a long time. Trouble was, their stars were too old, and their few promising youngsters were not yet stars.

Of the veterans, Reynolds was 40, Lopat, Johnny Sain and Rizzuto were 36, Enos Slaughter 38, Tommy Byrne 35, Jim Konstanty and Marlin Stuart 36.

One big trade changed the picture drastically, and put the Yankees back on top. From Baltimore they got pitchers Bob Turley and Don Larsen, and shortstop Billy Hunter, in exchange for six players they no longer needed. Hunter was a negligible part of the deal; the acquisition of Turley and Larsen, however, gave Ford much needed support on the mound.

In September of 1955, battling the Indians again for possession of first place, the Yankees got three tremendous pitching efforts from Whitey. On September 2 he threw a one-hit shutout against the Senators. Five days later he threw another one-hitter, this against Kansas City, becoming the fifth man in baseball history to throw successive one-hitters.

Then, in the final week of the season, he nailed down the pennant personally with a 3–1, five-hit victory over the White Sox. It was his eighteenth win of the season, against six defeats.

Whitey was now, percentage-wise, the most effective pitcher in baseball, with a four-season average of .735—61 wins and 22 losses.

He faced the Dodgers again in the 1955 World Series, a team known to be so deadly against left-handers that even the great Warren Spahn seldom pitched against them on their home grounds.

Whitey beat them twice, 6–5 and 5–1, striking out eight in the latter performance. The Dodgers won the Series, however, four games to three.

Now a new era in Yankee history began. Whitey, at 27, found himself suddenly the dean of the pitching staff. All the old-timers were gone with the exception of Tommy Byrne, who was used as a spot pitcher and relief man now. Otherwise, Larsen was 26, Grim, Turley and Bob Sturdivant were 25, newcomer Johnny Kucks was 22.

The rest of the team, too, had a younger look. Only Hank Bauer, 34, and Yogi Berra, 31, were over 30. The rest—Moose Skowron, Gil McDougald, Billy Martin, Mickey Mantle, Ellie Howard among the regulars, were under 30.

These new, younger Yankees had little trouble winning the 1956 pennant. An eleven-game winning streak in July broke open the pennant race. Capping the streak was another great Ford performance, a 2–0 shutout of Kansas City in which he struck out six straight to tie the American League record.

Still, his quest for a 20-game season was frustrated. With 19 under his belt he lost his last start, 1–0, to Baltimore.

The ability to handle adversity is one of the marks of a man. Whitey Ford, at the height of his illustrious career, exhibited such ability. During the 1957 season he developed a soreness in his shoulder that severely curtailed his effectiveness. He pitched most of the season in pain. At times he could not pitch at all without the aid of pain-killing injections and massage. He finished the season with an 11–5 record, the worst of his career.

Following a winter of rest and treatment at the famed Mayo Clinic, he began the 1958 season with a carefully prescribed regimen. He had to warm up longer than usual before each game, and warm up again briefly while the Yankees were batting—each inning!

Adhering to that schedule, he began the season in magnificent style. On June 2 he repeated his performance of striking out six men in a row, becoming the first man in baseball history to do so twice. In July he threw three straight shutouts. On August 8 he beat the Red Sox, 2–0, for his fourteenth victory and seventh shutout. He had lost only six.

Two days later, warming up in the bullpen to keep his shoulder loose, he began putting too much on the ball, and soon noticed that every time he threw a curve he began feeling pain again, this time in his elbow. In his next start, the elbow pain caught him as soon as he began pitching. Trying to rely on fast balls alone, he was quickly belted out of the box.

He didn't win another game all season. Only stalwart Yankee hitting kept him from worse than a 14–7 record. Still, his early season's work had been so remarkable he finished with a 2.01 earned-run average, to lead the league.

The Yankees managed to win the pennant, but the decline in the fortunes of both the team and Whitey that had begun in the latter half of 1958 continued in 1959. With disastrous results.

With his elbow and shoulder both plaguing him constantly, Whitey staggered through a 16–10 season. His 3.00 ERA was his worst since joining the Yankees. At that, his 16 victories was high for the staff, and might well have been higher with a little batting help. The 1959 Yankees were the hitless wonders. Little Bobby Richardson, the second baseman, was the team's slugger of the season with a .301 average.

All in all, the Yankees were hard pressed to finish third.

Again the Yankees resorted to a trade for help. And again they were successful. This time, in a massive exchange with Kansas City, they obtained outfielder Roger Maris. He hadn't done much for the Athletics, but with the Yankees he developed a punch that made him, with Mantle, the most sensational powerhouse duet since Lou Gehrig and Babe Ruth.

Whitey opened the 1960 season with a victory over the Orioles, but, ominously, had to withdraw after the seventh inning. His elbow was hurting again. After a week's rest he was knocked out in the first inning. He pitched sporadically over the next four months, winning five and losing five. In August, the Yankees were in second place. Then they dropped to third. The situation was becoming desperate.

Gritting his teeth against the pain, determined to halt

his team's skid, Whitey turned in a three-hit, 1–0 shutout, then with only two days' rest, badgered Stengel into letting him start against Baltimore.

Against his better judgment, Stengel gave him the ball. The Yankees needed every win they could get. Brilliantly Whitey came back with another 1–0, three-hit shutout. But after the game Paul Richards, the Orioles manager, sounded a note of warning. "Yes, Whitey really had his stuff today. But he may be sorry. You can't flout the laws of nature. He may feel the effects of this next time out."

Richards proved a prophet. Whitey couldn't even pitch a complete game for a month after that victory. Yet, when the time came, when the call came, when the chips were really down, he somehow mustered the strength and the courage he—and the Yankees—needed.

On September 16 the Orioles rode optimistically into New York for a climactic four-game series. They trailed the Yankees by one percentage point. Stengel now called on Whitey to pitch the opener, the game that would set the tone for the rest of the series, and undoubtedly bear heavily on the final outcome of the season.

Whitey gave the effort everything he had left. Though the strain on his ailing elbow caused the sweat to pour from his body and turn his pinstripes into a soaking, stained mess, he turned back the Orioles' challenge, 4–2. He actually had a shutout until he tired in the ninth inning.

Following his stirring performance, his teammates could do no less. Aroused to fighting pitch they swept the entire series from the Orioles. Not content with that, they went on to win fifteen straight games, a tremendous, unprecedented finish to another pennant-winning season.

A half-crippled Whitey Ford, with a 12–9 season's

record, showed them once again in the World Series that he could win the big ones. The Pittsburgh Pirates beat the Yankees for the World's Championship, but they couldn't touch Whitey. He shut them out twice.

Another new Yankee era was ushered in with the coming of spring, 1961. After the World Series loss to the Pirates, the Yankees had fired Casey Stengel, replacing him with Ralph Houk. During the winter months, the new skipper saw a lot of Whitey and catcher Yogi Berra, often dining and attending basketball games at Madison Square Garden together.

Of course, the team was often discussed. Down through the years, it had bothered Whitey that he had never won twenty games. To a considerable extent this was due to Stengel's strategy of skipping his turn against the poorer clubs when an important series was slated next against a tough club. As a result, Whitey lost many starting chances that probably would have resulted in victories.

He and Berra both talked to Houk about this. Actually, despite his elbow and shoulder trouble, Whitey felt he was most effective when he pitched every fourth day, regardless of the opponent, regardless of how he felt. Berra agreed with him. A number of discussions with their new manager seemed to be getting nowhere, however, until one night at a basketball game Houk said to Whitey:

"Look, you think you can do your best pitching every fourth day, and I think you can do your best pitching every fourth day. So, let's consider that settled."

There was a new look to baseball that year. The leagues had expanded to ten teams each. In the American League there were now the Los Angeles Angels and the Minnesota Twins. It was against those Twins (actually, the old Washington Senators in a new home) that Whitey began the new season under a new pilot.

The start was a bad one. He lost to the Twins, 6–0. But then it was six weeks before he lost another game, racking up six straight victories before the Red Sox beat him, 2–1.

Now a new, very definite pattern had evolved in his pitching. He was starting more often, but finishing less. Every time he got into trouble—even mild trouble—Luis Arroyo, the team's new bullpen hero, took over. The New York sportswriters took this to be a symptom of Whitey's recurrent arm trouble. Manager Houk, however, explained it as strategy.

"Whitey always paced himself to go nine. But now that I'm letting him pitch every fourth day, he doesn't need to pace himself. I want him to pitch as hard as he can for as long as he can. With Arroyo in the bullpen we have the best short relief man in the business."

In this fashion Whitey had ten victories by mid-June. Normally he would have had just ten starts by then; this time he had been given fifteen.

"More starts, more wins," he told the sportswriters.

"How about the sore arm you're supposed to have?" one reporter questioned.

"It's still sore," replied Whitey. "Dieting, care and regular work help. Sure, it hurts every time I pitch. But I've learned that you just have to go out and pitch, pain or not, as long as it doesn't hurt so bad you can't throw effectively."

On August 10, beating the Angels 3–1 for his fourteenth straight victory, Whitey finally realized his ambition. The win was his twentieth of the season. He went on for a 25–4 finish, the best won-lost record in Yankee history. His 210 strikeouts was also a club record for a left-hander.

Having won the pennant for their new manager, the Yankees then set out to give him his first World's Championship. Facing them in the World Series were the Cincinnati Reds. Surprise winners in the National League, they were heavy underdogs against the Yankee powerhouse.

In the opener Whitey made the odds stand up, shutting them out, 2–0, on two hits. Counting his two straight shutouts over the Pirates the year before, this gave him 27 straight World Series shutout innings, just two less than the record set by Babe Ruth in the years 1916–18.

After a two-game rest, he returned to action. He got through the first two innings unscored upon, to tie the record. Then he blanked the Reds in the third, to set a new record. On he rolled, through five shutout innings. But, in the fifth, while batting, he had fouled a ball painfully off his foot. When Elio Chacon opened the Reds' sixth with a single, Whitey ran to cover first, limping badly. At once Houk removed him from the game.

As he trotted to the dugout, thunderous applause rolled down from the Crosley Field grandstands. Even the Cincinnati partisans were paying homage to his new World Series record of 32 consecutive scoreless innings.

He left with a 4–0 lead, which the Yankees extended finally to 7–0. This gave him another World Series record of nine victories.

After the Yankees clinched the title with a 13–5 rout in the final game, the awards and the honors began to descend upon Whitey. For his pitching in the World Series he received two awards. *Sport* magazine gave him a Corvette sports car as the outstanding performer. The

New York sportswriters gave him the Babe Ruth Award.
Then he won the most important of them all to a pitcher—the Cy Young Award.

A serious recurrence of shoulder trouble caught up with Whitey the following season. Still, he managed a fine 17-8 season, ran his World Series records to 33⅔ scoreless innings and 10 victories as the Yankees beat the Giants.

"I guess that one will stand up for a while," quipped Whitey afterward. "Just how many guys ever get a chance to start 22 games in a Series?"

Though still battling the recurrent shoulder pains, Whitey pitched superbly in 1963. Injuries to Mantle and Maris had weakened the Yankees seriously, and, without Ford's 24-7 record, they could never have won another pennant.

As pitching won them the pennant, so did pitching beat them in the World Series. The Dodgers, with the best mound staff in baseball, trounced them four straight. In the finale, Whitey lost to Sandy Koufax, 2-1, though throwing a two-hitter.

Again the Yankees changed managers. Houk was moved up to general manager, and Yogi Berra was made manager. At once Yogi made his old friend and roommate Whitey a pitching coach. It was rare for an active pitcher to take on such a time-consuming chore. However, Whitey was anxious to see his friend make good. He accepted the post.

Until July, all seemed well. The team was hitting. Whitey was leading an effective mound staff. Then Mantle hurt his knee. Whitey hurt his hip and missed a few turns. The bullpen corps came up with an epidemic of sore arms.

In August, trailing the Orioles by six games, the team

rallied. Whitey led the way with key victories. However, toward the latter part of August, he began suffering from a numbness in the fingers of his left hand. He found it difficult to grip the ball properly in the late innings. He told no one about his problem, but continued to take his regular turn in the pitching rotation.

Only after the Yankees passed the Orioles and clinched the pennant did he reveal that he would need a postseason operation. Despite the numbness in his fingers, he compiled a 17–6 record in 1964.

He hoped he could suffer through the World Series, but he lasted just until the sixth inning of the opener against the Cardinals, then left and pitched no more. Without him the Yankees lost their second straight Series.

The closing of the 1964 season, on a disappointing note, seemed to signal the beginning of the end of the Yankee dynasty that had ruled the league for so many years. Like a punctured balloon, the Yankees suddenly collapsed. In 1965 Johnny Keane, who had beaten them in the Series as Cardinals' manager, took over the reins from Berra. Yogi was fired, and went to the New York Mets as a coach.

Unfortunately for Keane, he took the reins on a crippled horse. The great Yankee stars had already seen their best years. Mantle, Maris, Howard and Ford, on the downhill slope of their playing careers, suffered early season injuries. Whitey's shoulder began bothering him again. After a terrible start, he came back to finish with a 16–13 record. But the Yankees straggled home sixth.

The following season completed the debacle. Shortly after it began, the Yankees disintegrated completely. Nobody, not even Mantle, was hitting. Whitey, for so long the heart and muscle of the mound corps, was clearly pitching out of the well of his experience, relying on craft and courage. In a move born of desperation, the Yankees fired the unfortunate Keane and put Houk back in the field manager's spot.

The team needed more than a new guiding hand. It needed new talent, new blood to replace the tired and battle-worn stars who had once commanded terror around the league. Some promising youngsters the Yankees did possess, but they were years away from stardom, if they would ever make those exalted heights at all.

With these, and the tattered remains of the old Yankees, Houk could accomplish little. The team finished last in 1966.

Pitching just 73 innings, a weary Whitey won 2 and lost 5.

This was indeed the handwriting on the wall for him. He had no desire to hang on to the end, a washed-up spot pitcher, bottom man on the bullpen brigade. There was some consideration over the winter months that another operation might prolong his career. But he wasn't sure he could go through another operation, or even that he wanted to pitch again.

However, for his own pride, and for all the things the Yankees had meant to him for the past fifteen years, he gave it another try. In spring training there were brief flashes of his old form, but soon after the 1967 season began, he realized he was through. A new bone spur on his left elbow was the final blow. His stuff was gone. His arm was dead.

And so, before a Memorial Day doubleheader at Yankee Stadium, Whitey announced to the thousands in the stands that he was retiring.

It was a sad day for baseball. There was the realization that with the close of Whitey Ford's brilliant career

Whitey Ford

there ended, too, a glowing chapter in the history of the game. Baseball would be the less without him.

Club president Michael Burke summed up the Yankees' feelings on that Memorial Day when he said: "As far as we are concerned, we hope Whitey Ford will be a Yankee forever."

He remained with the team as pitching coach through the 1968 season. Then he announced that he was retiring from baseball completely. Everyone connected with the game hoped it would be just temporary. Somewhere, it was hoped, Whitey would find a place in baseball that would suit his talents and his needs.

Whitey retired with imposing credentials that will lead him to the Hall of Fame someday. The Yankees' record-holding winner, with 236 victories, he was an All-Star eight times, held World Series records difficult to surpass, and was considered one of the gamest competitors of all time.

Sandy Koufax

Sandy Koufax ●●●●●●●●●●●●●●●●●●●●●●●●●●●●●

From the Parade Grounds in Brooklyn to the site where Ebbets Field used to stand is a brisk walk of perhaps half an hour. Once, a long time ago, when the Dodgers were known affectionately as The Bums and were the darlings of all Brooklyn, that brief distance was often measured in years. Traversed in dreams.

A vast rectangular playing field set in the heart of a middle-class residential area, the Parade Grounds are so huge several games at once can be played without confusion. Down through the decades, thousands of Brooklyn boys have scampered over the dirt and the grass, baseball season dissolving into football season and then reappearing, the crack of the bat sounding even before the last pass has been thrown in the late winter sunshine.

Of those thousands, uncounted scores have dreamed of the triumphant march from sandlot to stadium. Very few really felt they heard the call. Even fewer answered the trumpet. One or two stayed for the game.

Sandy Koufax was one.

Sandy was a true product of Brooklyn—the Brooklyn of the years just after World War II. Sports and schooling were uppermost in his mind, and were joined together in practical harmony. At Lafayette High School, and at the neighborhood Jewish Community House, Sandy was a topnotch basketball player. He was big and fast and especially noted as an accurate passer. Basketball was more than just a sport to Sandy, however. He saw it as a means to an end—college, a basketball scholarship to a leading university, where he might pursue his interest in architecture.

Baseball—well, what boy in Brooklyn in the early 1950's wasn't interested in baseball? The sandlots were disappearing quickly in the postwar building boom, but every patch of ground large enough—and some not large enough—was sure to be covered by boys playing baseball from early spring to late winter. If it wasn't baseball it was softball or stickball; if it wasn't a field it was a street or a schoolyard. But in Brooklyn then, a bunch of boys, a ball of any description and a stick of some kind meant a ball game.

Sandy was good enough to rate a place on an amateur team, the Parkviews, who played in the Coney Island League and at the Parade Grounds. As Bettsyhead Park and Bushwick Park had been the centers of Brooklyn amateur league baseball in the early 1940's, so had the Parade Grounds become the center after the war.

Major league scouts descended upon the Parade Grounds like flies on a sugar cube. A flow of young talent was constantly needed to fill the rosters of the minor league clubs, even if many of those pulled off the sandlots never got out of Class A ball.

Sandy was a catcher on the Parkviews. He didn't take baseball seriously; that is, he didn't consider it as a career, or the Parkviews as a steppingstone to greater things. Baseball was fun. In any case, he didn't think that he was by any stretch of the imagination a good enough catcher to play professionally.

However, as happens in life, accident turns the commonplace into rarity, happenstance into history, and desperation into genius.

In the course of a doubleheader at the Parade Grounds one Sunday afternoon, the Parkviews found themselves short a pitcher. It was recalled that Sandy Koufax could throw hard. He was pressed into service as a pitcher.

From the opening strokes of his mighty left arm it was apparent that Sandy could throw hard indeed. However, where the ball would land once it left his hand—that was another story. He was the fastest pitcher on the Parade Grounds and the wildest. He struck out a lot of batters, but he walked more. He didn't always win, but he was spectacular even when he lost.

Strikeouts in large numbers are impressive, even in the sandlot leagues. The young pitcher with the high hard one that he can blow past the hitters is the one likely to catch the eye of the big league scouts. His performances will tend to eclipse those of a pitcher who wins more games but does so with craft and control and curves. It happened in the case of Whitey Ford.

Sandy discovered that he liked pitching. He liked the feeling of control over the game, the complete participation. A greater awareness of the potentialities of baseball grew within him; in his senior year at Lafayette High he pitched for the school baseball team.

In the spring of 1953 the scouts began to look him over carefully. Only the Phillies made him an offer, however. Sandy thought about it briefly, discussed the offer with his parents, and declined. He didn't relish the thought of pitching in obscurity on a Phillies' farm team.

He refused the offer not so much because it wasn't good enough, not because he thought he was better than a farm team pitcher, but because he had a more attractive alternative. The University of Cincinnati offered him an athletic scholarship on the basis of his basketball talents. To Sandy and his parents, steeped in the traditions of education, this made more sense than pitching for someplace like Tidewater or Spartanburg or wherever it was the Phils had in mind in their farm system.

He entered the University in 1953. However, the Phillies had seriously stirred in Sandy the idea that professional baseball might be his calling after all. He had no strong leanings toward any other profession, no deep academic interest. Architecture, which he planned to study at Cincinnati, was more a chosen vocation than a dedication.

Sandy made a decision. He would turn pro, but only if a club offered a large enough bonus to cover the cost of a four-year college education—in case he failed to make the grade in baseball.

Meantime he attended classes and played basketball. As a freshman he averaged ten points a game. His coach considered him a first-rate prospect for the varsity. Until then, there was the baseball season to consider. In Cincinnati on a basketball scholarship, Sandy needn't have played baseball. However, the basketball coach was also the baseball coach, and the transition was a natural one.

Sandy was an immediate sensation. In two consecutive games he struck out a total of 34 men, then 51 men in 32 innings. He also walked 30 at the same time. Again, the strikeouts attracted attention. A scout from the Cincinnati Reds watched him for a while. He reported back that Sandy was too wild to merit consideration.

Major league teams don't cool quickly on young pitchers who throw as hard as Sandy did. Once they've fingered such a man they watch awhile and wait. Control and a curve can often be learned. A fast ball you either have or you don't.

When school was out and Sandy returned to New York for the summer the Giants asked him to appear for a tryout. He took the subway up to the Polo Grounds, suited up, was given the ball and told to loosen up. Bobby Hofman was there to catch him.

Sandy was nervous. Overanxious. He knew all eyes were on his vaunted fast ball. He wound up and threw as hard as he could. The ball flew high over Hofman's head and hit the grandstand on the fly. Now even further unnerved, Sandy gave the wooden boards a fearful beating, while Hofman got few pitches in the neighborhood of his mitt.

The Giants lost all interest.

But other scouts came around. They are a clever, competitive lot, major league scouts. Their jobs depend on their ability to unearth future stars. The better scouts have the tenacity of a bloodhound and the guile of a fox. From experience they know that other scouts will feign loss of interest in a youngster to discourage interest by rivals, thus smoothing their own negotiations. They also are well aware of the fact that many a major league star was passed over by a succession of scouts when first discovered, only to be signed later by a more discerning one. Furthermore, a boy might look terrible in one tryout, but marvelous in the next one.

Thus, the Giants' verdict against Sandy did not discourage other teams. The Pirates, the Dodgers and the Braves had a look at him that same summer. The Pirates made the first offer, but hesitated at meeting Sandy's bonus demands. It wasn't the amount of money that stalled them. It was the bonus rule.

As this rule stood at the time, a major league team signing a boy for a bonus in excess of $4000 had to keep him on their roster for two years. They could not send him directly to a farm team. The rule was adopted deliberately to discourage astronomical bonuses, to give the poorer clubs a fairer chance to sign young talent. Naturally any team would think twice before signing an amateur and bringing him directly to the major leagues. No matter how talented, an amateur needed to gain experience in the minors. In the few cases where a club felt it necessary to buy a player at any cost, the "bonus baby," as he was termed, found himself collecting splinters on the bench when he should have been playing in the minors and learning.

A promising young talent could be ruined in such a manner. Many baseball observers agree that pitcher Johnny Antonelli, a Braves "bonus baby" of 1948, had a fine future spoiled that way. And it very nearly happened to Sandy Koufax.

Eventually that summer both the Pirates and the Braves decided they would take the chance and give Sandy a big bonus to sign. But while they were busy considering, scout Al Campanis of the Dodgers slipped in with a definite offer of $14,000. Sandy accepted the offer.

He returned to school in September without actually signing a contract. When they learned this, the Braves and the Pirates chased him with bigger numbers. However, Sandy had given his word to Campanis. He stood by that. In December, he signed. He was officially a member of the Brooklyn Dodgers.

From Parade Grounds to Ebbets Field in one easy giant step. Now it remained to be seen if the boots fit.

Reporting to spring training as a Dodger in 1955 was an indescribable thrill for a Brooklyn lad of nineteen. It would have been so in any era, but in addition, this was one of the great teams of Dodger history. Sandy was joining a pitching staff headed by Don Newcombe, Johnny Podres, Carl Erskine, Billy Loes and Clem Labine. At first base was Gil Hodges, at second, Junior Gilliam, shortstop Pee Wee Reese, third base Jackie Robinson;

Duke Snider, Carl Furillo and Sandy Amoros patrolled the outfield. Catching was the immortal Roy Campanella.

This was a team that had won two pennants in the last three seasons, losing the year before to the Giants by one game.

A marvelous aggregation. A superb pitching staff. It was a supreme honor for an amateur like Sandy to wear the same uniform and share the clubhouse.

At the same time it meant they didn't need help from a "bonus baby" like him. The Dodgers welcomed Sandy with a uniform, a locker, and a piece of bench to call his own.

Some seasons later Joe Becker, the Dodgers' pitching coach, told a sportswriter, "Sandy would have been a top star twice as fast had he been able to pitch regularly in the minors or with a weaker club in the majors."

Toward the end of June, Sandy got his first chance. By then the Dodgers had a fourteen-game lead and could afford to experiment. He came on in relief one night in Milwaukee and pitched two good innings before being removed for a pinch hitter. Another good relief job earned him a start, against the Pirates. As expected, he was wild and fast.

The Pirates didn't hit him hard, but his wildness kept the bases occupied behind him. Then, he showed his inexperience by trying to pitch even harder with men on base. The harder he threw, the wilder he became. In the fifth inning he was relieved, having given up one run and three hits, but eight walks.

In August, more than a month later, manager Alston let him pitch again. The pennant was all but won, the pitchers were in need of extra rest. Alston gave him the ball against Cincinnati.

The Reds were no pushover team. They could hit. Sluggers like Ted Kluszewski, Gus Bell and Wally Post could break open a game with one swat of the bat. Against this crew Sandy felt somewhat less than confident. He hadn't worked in a month. He felt tight and nervous.

He got through the first inning easily enough, which settled his nerves and restored his confidence. When he came out for the second he was determined to take his time and concentrate on getting the ball over the plate. With Campanella chirping encouragement behind the plate, Sandy went briskly to work.

He was as fast as always, and now he was hitting the strike zone as well. As the game wore on, and his confidence grew, he began to get more calls from Campy for his curve. He hit the target with those, too, upsetting the Cincinnati hitters who were digging in for his fast ball.

On the mound for the last half of the ninth, sitting comfortably on a 7–0 lead, Sandy had the feeling he had struck out quite a few Cincinnati batters. He took a look out at the scoreboard and noted, too, that he had given up just one hit. In the depths of his concentration he hadn't quite kept count, but was aware that he had been pitching an exceptional game.

He gave up one more hit in the ninth, then wrapped up his first major league victory, a 7–0 two-hitter. He struck out fourteen men, including the dangerous Gus Bell four straight times.

Without question this was a spectacular performance for a nineteen-year-old pitcher fresh off the sandlots. But wisened baseball men nodded their heads in wait-and-see attitude. Many a rookie pitcher had displayed early mastery over the league's leading hitters, only to have those same serves blasted off the fences the second time around.

The Dodgers needed only to look back at the previous September, when a rookie fresh up from the minor leagues named Karl Spooner pitched shutouts the first two times he was given the ball. Then he faded as quickly as he had blossomed.

Sandy had a long road to travel before he could be considered a reliable major league pitcher. Four days after his shutout of the Reds he pitched an inning of relief and was routed with four runs and five hits. He followed that with a shutout of the Pirates, then lost his next two games.

He was inconsistent. His 2–2 record for 1955, with 30 strikeouts and 28 walks in 42 innings, only indicated to the Dodgers something they knew when they signed him. He was fast but he was wild. He was either very good or very bad.

The cure for a talented young pitcher with such a problem can often be found with constant work. But Sandy was a bonus baby. He couldn't get work. Over the next two seasons he pitched sporadically. Alston considered him to be unreliable, which in fact he was, good for odd relief jobs in lopsided ball games or the occasional start when doubleheaders pressured the mound staff.

The situation was not an uncommon one in baseball, applying to veteran and newcomer alike who are trying to win a job. It was like the question of which came first, the chicken or the egg. Sandy would complain to Buzzy Bavasi, the general manager: "I want to pitch and I'm not getting a chance."

Bavasi would answer: "How can you pitch when you can't get the side out?"

And Sandy would reply: "How can I get the side out when I don't pitch?"

The professional athlete, no matter his game, needs

constant competition to keep his reflexes sharp and his skills at the ready. If he is relegated to the sidelines, when he is finally called upon in a spot to pinch-hit, to pitch, or throw a pass or sink a basket, he will often look bad—and thus be returned for another long stretch on the sidelines. It's a self-perpetuating waste of talent, but often there is no immediate solution.

Patiently, Sandy waited. He was still young. So long as the Dodgers didn't give up on him, he would not give up on the Dodgers. When the club announced that it was moving to Los Angeles at the end of the 1957 season, Sandy hoped that the change in environment would bring with it a change in his fortunes.

The Dodgers did not do well their opening season in Los Angeles. The stadium was not suited to their hitters or to their pitchers. In addition, their stars were old, many of them in the final stages of their careers. The team spent the season struggling in the second division.

Sandy at least derived some benefit from the team's collapse. Under the circumstances, Alston thought it a good time to give his scatter-armed young hurler more work. Sandy soon found himself starting as well as relieving. On one road trip he appeared in five straight games and seven of eleven.

As he had always maintained it would, the constant work helped. He won regularly, pitching fine ball. He was 7–3 until he was spiked in the ankle on a play at first base. The injury benched him for two weeks; when he went back to work, his winning touch was gone.

Nobody knew what was wrong, but he just wasn't getting the ball over; or, if he got it over the plate, there was nothing on the pitch. Perhaps, favoring the injured ankle, he was striding badly. Perhaps the layoff had cooled his arm. Whatever the reason, he developed control trouble again, and he was being hit hard. Naturally, the worse he pitched, the harder he pressed; the more he pressed, the worse he got.

He completed the 1958 season with an 11–11 record. In 159 innings he struck out 131. And issued 105 walks.

His bad habits continued on into the beginning of the 1959 season. Five straight times he was knocked out of the box, giving up 15 runs and 17 walks in his first 11 innings pitched. Then, suddenly and for no apparent reason, he experienced a complete reversal of form. He won three straight starts, in one game striking out 16—one less than Dizzy Dean's National League record, two less than Bob Feller's major league mark.

His three straight wins were not enough to convince Alston that he could be relied upon. His record showed too many inconsistencies. The Dodgers were in a tough seesaw battle with the Giants for first place, and Alston was playing each game as though it were the pennant-clincher. Whenever Sandy appeared to be in the least bit of trouble, therefore, he was pulled out promptly. He didn't finish or win another game until mid-August. He beat the Phillies, 8–2, striking out 13 men.

That performance earned him a shot at the Giants a week later. San Francisco had a two-game lead, with the final month of competition about to begin. Sandy's start was a crucial one; it meant opening September's campaign either one game behind the Giants—or three behind.

Sandy struck out the first two Giants. But Willie Mays doubled and Orlando Cepeda doubled him home before Sandy got the third out. Alston sent the bullpen into action. An inning later he told them to sit down. Koufax was in control. His fast ball was popping, and his curve broke sharply and true. He had the big Giant hitters flailing at air.

Willie McCovey broke through for a homer in the fifth inning, otherwise Sandy was virtually untouchable.

As he walked out to the mound in Los Angeles Coliseum to pitch the top of the ninth, he had 15 strikeouts, and a 2-2 tie.

Eddie Bressoud faced him in the batter's box. Sandy struck out the shortstop on four pitches. Second baseman Danny O'Connell worked the count to two-and-two, then watched a third strike go by. That gave Sandy 17 strikeouts to tie Dizzy Dean's National League record.

Now came Jack Sanford, the Giants' pitcher. Sandy wasted no time on him. Three fast balls whizzed by Sanford's waving bat. Eighteen strikeouts! A new National League record, and Sandy had tied the major league record! To do it, he had struck out 15 of the last 17 men he faced.

To complete the picture, Wally Moon homered with two on in the bottom of the ninth (including Sandy, who had singled) for a 5-2 victory.

Together with his 13 strikeouts against the Phils the week before, Sandy had 31 for two straight games, another new major league record. Then, in his next start, he struck out 10 more, while losing, 3-0. This set a new major league record of 41 strikeouts in three consecutive games, surpassing the previous mark of 38 held jointly by Walter Johnson and Bob Feller.

Sandy had come back well after his terrible start that season. He finished with an 8-6 record, and a career high of 173 strikeouts in 153 innings.

Alston thought well enough of him now to start him in the World Series. He pitched the fifth game, and turned in an excellent performance. But the Dodgers gave him no hitting support. He left after seven innings, losing 1–0, and eventually was charged with the loss.

Still, he had shown that he was maturing into a solid, dependable pitcher. Sandy and the Dodgers looked forward optimistically to the 1960 season.

It turned out to be a disaster. He won 8 and lost 13. At the end of the season he gave serious thought to quitting baseball. He was only twenty-five, he could still go back to college, or go into business. Perhaps, with his baseball contacts and reputation, he might do something connected with the game.

What was especially frustrating to him was that several times he seemed so close to making the big breakthrough, so close to realizing his obvious potential. Yet each time, for no specific reason anyone could pinpoint, he relapsed into wildness and ineffectiveness.

He vowed to give baseball just one more season. If he failed again, that was it.

Of course, the Dodgers were as frustrated and as puzzled as he was. The only criticism of merit they could make of his pitching was that he had the habit of trying too hard, of trying to overpower the hitters. It can work on the sandlots and even in minor league baseball. But not in the big leagues.

In Florida, that spring of 1961, manager Alston sent Koufax one day to pitch with the Dodgers' B team, against the Twins. On the short plane ride to the Twins' training camp, Sandy sat and chatted with Norm Sherry, the club's third-string catcher. In the course of the conversation Sherry said to him:

"Listen, Sandy, this is just an exhibition game. Why don't you ease up a bit, throw naturally? Instead of forcing the fast ball, I think if you just concentrated on getting the ball over, your troubles would be over. You've got enough natural speed to do it."

Sandy thought a moment. Then he shrugged. "Why not?" he said. "What have I got to lose?"

This was early in spring training, and he found that he was still a bit off the mark. He walked five Twins batters, but he pitched seven innings of no-hit ball. Moreover, following Sherry's advice, he restrained himself with men on base. Instead of following his usual pattern of throwing harder in the jams, he coolly threw to spots—and he got the hitters out.

At once Sandy saw that this was what he had been searching for. This appeared to be the solution to his control problem, indeed to all his problems.

Although he lost his first game, to the Pirates, he didn't waver. He beat Cincinnati his next time out, the first time he had ever won a game in April. Then he won six straight, was 10–3 in July, and for the first time in his career was picked for the All-Star Team.

Sandy Koufax had become a pitcher.

Lack of hitting support and a temporary relapse into his old ways kept his season's record to 18–13. This was more than just a professional performance, however. It was another record-breaker. In his last start he lost to the Phillies, 2–1, striking out seven men. That gave him 269 strikeouts for the season, a new National League record, two better than Christy Mathewson's old mark.

The sad part of Sandy's astounding career was that just at the moment he developed into the best pitcher in baseball, one of the greatest ever, in fact, he was attacked by physical forces that were to shorten his baseball life.

In 1962 he began by winning four games in April. One of the victories was another record-setter. On April 24, he struck out 18 Cubs in a 10–2 victory to become the only man in baseball ever to strike out 18 men twice.

Toward the middle of May, while pitching against

the Mets, he noticed a peculiar numbness in his left index finger. Day after day the numbness spread; the finger became cold and lifeless. Sandy ignored the abnormality. He was pitching the best ball of his life, the numbness didn't interfere with his throwing, so—why complain, he thought.

On June 30, pitching with a completely numb finger, he pitched the first no-hitter of his career, against the Mets. He had in fact given up just three earned runs in his last five starts, and already had 11 victories.

The next time he started, against the Giants, the numb finger turned red, and began to throb with pain. Sandy found it impossible to throw a curve. Relying solely on his fast ball, he had a two-hitter going when he had to quit in the ninth inning. The agony was unbearable.

The Dodgers' doctor advised Sandy to see a vascular specialist, diagnosing a serious circulation problem. However, since there didn't appear to be any immediate danger, Sandy put off further examination. He wanted to make the All-Star Game in Washington. After that, he joined the team on its road trip.

Now the finger turned blue. A blood blister developed which split the first time he threw the ball. When the Reds belted him out in the first inning he decided it was time he had the finger thoroughly examined.

The vascular specialists he saw were amazed that he had been able to pitch at all, much less pitch so spectacularly. They discovered, in the area between his thumb and index finger, what appeared to be a giant arterial blood clot that almost completely cut off circulation.

Had he waited a few more days before seeking treatment, they told him, gangrene would have set in.

"We would have had no choice," a doctor told him. "The finger would have had to come off."

Weeks of intense treatment with drugs and ointments

and injections arrested the infection. Gradually, the circulation returned.

Without Sandy, the Dodgers didn't stand a chance. The strain on the pitching staff told eventually. When he finally returned to action, it was almost like spring training all over again; it took time to get back into shape. He tried too hard too soon and was hit hard. The Dodgers lost the pennant. Sandy's brilliant beginning was reduced to a 14–7 finish, but his 2.54 earned-run average led the league.

Again Sandy felt the pangs of discouragement. Again, he had come so close, only to miss out on a great season. True, he had shown that when he was physically right, there wasn't a better pitcher in baseball. But— would he be one of those hurlers destined to be forever on the threshold of stardom, held back by chronic injury?

He and the Dodgers anxiously awaited the answer. Without him, the weak-hitting team was just a second-division club.

Everyone breathed a little easier when he started the second contest of the 1963 season and beat the Cubs with a five-hitter, 2–1. Then he struck out 14 in the process of winning a two-hitter. A torn shoulder membrane kept him out of action for two weeks, but he came right back to beat the Cardinals.

On May 11, at Dodger Stadium, he faced the Giants. Harvey Kuenn, the leadoff hitter, hit a line drive to deep center field, but Willie Davis gathered it in. That was the hardest hit ball off Sandy all night. He retired twenty-two straight batters before walking catcher Ed Bailey in the eighth. In the ninth he walked McCovey. Those were the only two Giants to reach base.

A second no-hitter for Sandy!

Sandy Koufax

This one gave him special satisfaction. A year earlier, when he no-hit the Mets, there were some shrugs of dismissal. "The Mets. Big deal!"

This time it was the Giants, one of the powerhouse teams in the league.

After that, Sandy just kept on rolling. He demonstrated at last the true, consistent greatness of his fabulous left arm. He won 25 games to lead the league, losing only 5. His 1.88 ERA was also best in the league. He beat his own strikeout record with 306. He won his first MVP Award, and then the Cy Young Award as the best pitcher in the major leagues.

To top off the season, he beat the Yankees twice in the World Series, 5–2 and 2–1, as the Dodgers took the Yankees four straight. He struck out 23 men in the two games, 15 in the first for a new World Series strikeout record.

Koufax, the unquestioned strikeout king of baseball, continued his magic into the 1964 season. He pitched a no-hitter for the third successive season, won 15 out of 16 games going into mid-August, and appeared headed for new heights of success.

Then, in Milwaukee one day, leading off second base, Tony Cloninger tried to pick him off. He dived back safely, hurting his left elbow slightly in the process. He rubbed it gingerly, noticing a small lump. The elbow felt stiff when he resumed pitching, but it didn't interfere with his game. He forgot about the incident.

When he awoke the next morning the elbow was so swollen he could barely move the arm.

A series of extensive examinations revealed a serious situation. Sandy had traumatic arthritis of the left elbow; it would never be cured. Apparently the injury suffered in sliding had merely triggered, had hastened an already degenerative process brought about by the steady wear and tear of pitching. Further throwing was possible under constant care and treatment, but it would aggravate the condition. In any case, Sandy was through pitching for 1964. At the time, August 16, he had a 19–5 record.

He was told that he must rest the arm completely all through the winter. Then, whether or not he would ever pitch again would depend on how the elbow responded to rest and subsequent treatment. Spring training, 1965, would spell out the verdict.

In his heart and in his mind, Sandy was determined to pitch. He now had a bagful of records, an MVP Award, a Cy Young Award and recognition as one of the all-time masters of the mound. Yet he had only one season in which he had won more than 20 games, even more remarkable testimony to the brilliance he had evidenced in the space of a few years.

He had to prove that the records, the awards, were not the result of a brief flash of brilliance, were not evidences of a "fluke" streak of luck, of a series of coincidences. The only way he could prove that he merited the adulation and the superlative adjectives was to come back and do it again—and even better than ever before.

It was with these thoughts in mind that Sandy Koufax began spring training in 1965.

He discovered, strangely and ominously, that when he worked out on the mound, the elbow didn't bother him. However, immediately afterward it would swell and throb with pain. Since this had been termed an incurable part of his arthritis, Sandy and the Dodger trainers devised a system that would at least keep his left arm in working condition.

After each game, Sandy had to soak his elbow in a tub of ice for an hour or so, to prevent swelling. The ice

Sandy Koufax

made his skin peel, so a rubber, later a cellophane, sleeve was designed to protect the skin while allowing the freezing to take effect.

The system worked. Sandy was the medical miracle of 1965—and the pitching miracle. He threw better than ever. His control was sharp. His fast ball moved. His curve tied the hitters in knots.

"What sore arm?" asked the league's sluggers, flailing at thin air.

He was 6–2, with three straight wins, when he lost a 2–1 decision to St. Louis on May 26. On May 30 he beat the Reds, 12–5, then won another ten straight games before the Reds beat him, 4–1.

Rushing into September in a four-way pennant race were the Giants, Dodgers, Reds and Braves. With 21 victories and 7 defeats, Sandy, backed up by Don Drysdale, kept the Dodgers in the thick of the fight.

On September 9, the Cubs arrived at Dodger Stadium for a single game. Sandy was given the ball.

His stuff didn't look good when he began; it hadn't looked good in his last four starts. Three of them he had lost, two by one-run margins. His fast ball wasn't moving, didn't have the hop. Quickly, against the Cubs, Sandy switched to his curve, and got the hitters out.

For Chicago, pitcher Bob Hendley was doing the same.

In the fifth inning, the weak-hitting Dodgers scored in typical fashion. Lou Johnson walked, was sacrificed to second, stole third and raced home when the throw went wild into left field.

Working carefully on the one-run lead, Sandy discovered that the fast ball had come alive again. He switched off the curve, and the move added to the futility already felt by the Cub hitters.

They couldn't touch him. Couldn't get a man on base.

With two out in the seventh, Sandy went to three balls and no strikes on Billy Williams.

He knew where he stood. He didn't need to look at the scoreboard. He remembered how two walks had ruined his near-perfect game against the Giants.

He bore down hard on Williams, blew two fast balls by him. Then the Chicago outfielder lifted a soft fly ball to Johnson to end the inning.

That was the last chance any Dodger had at a batted ball.

Now Sandy gave the appearance of a fantastically tuned machine. Working smoothly, gracefully, without hurry, he struck out Ron Santo, Ernie Banks and Byron Browne in the eighth inning.

In the ninth inning he struck out Chris Krug. Joe Amalfitano came up to pitch-hit. Sandy struck him out. Harvey Kuenn came up to pinch-hit. Sandy struck him out.

A perfect game! Fourteen strikeouts!

This 1–0 no-hitter was his fourth, giving him the distinction of being the only man in baseball history to throw four no-hitters. And Sandy did the trick in successive seasons.

Following that contest, he lost a 2–1 decision to the Cubs, threw three straight shutouts, then beat Milwaukee, 3–1, to finish with a 26–8 record.

He led the major leagues in everything that mattered. His 26 victories was tops, accomplished in 27 complete games, 336 innings, and with a 2.04 ERA. His 382 strikeouts was a new major league record, far surpassing Feller's 348. Again he won the Cy Young Award as the best pitcher in baseball.

In the World Series he shut out the Twins twice to help the Dodgers to the World's Championship.

And the elbow? As the doctors had warned him, continued pitching, while possible, could only aggravate the condition. Through the 1966 season, while he continued to demonstrate, over and over, his incredible talents, the elbow's condition deteriorated.

How he managed to pitch was a mystery. That he won, and won regularly in spectacular style, was a miracle—or, perhaps, a triumph of will over pain and adversity.

Sandy was so good, baseball observers agreed that each time he pitched it was expected that he would win. Many of the games he lost were low-run contests, by a one-run margin. At times, watching him work, the fast ball exploding, the curve twisting the hitters into knots, one wondered how anybody ever hit him at all. Had he thrown no-hitters all the time, few would have been more than mildly amazed.

In 1966, with his elbow worse than ever, he pitched the Dodgers to another pennant. He won 27 games, again led the league in strikeouts, and won his third successive Cy Young Award.

But the effort cost him dearly. Only Sandy himself could say exactly how much it cost him in pain, in anxiety. No one, not even the doctors, could say what it cost him in atrophy of his arthritic elbow, nor could anyone predict accurately what further pitching might do to his left arm, to his entire body.

He had proven, as he felt it important to prove, that he was more than one of the best pitchers who ever lived. He proved that he had pride, that he had courage, that he had loyalty to his team and to all those who had shown their faith in him.

Shortly after the Dodgers lost the World Series to Baltimore in 1966, Sandy announced his retirement.

"I don't want to take the chance of disabling myself," he said. "It's got to the point where I was told I could do permanent damage if I continued to pitch. I decided I have a lot of years left after baseball, and I want to live them with the full use of my body."

Soon afterward, he became a sportscaster on radio and television. In time, he will find his deserved niche in baseball's Hall of Fame.

Many fine and gracious compliments have been paid Sandy Koufax during his career and upon his retirement.

Summing them up best of all was the editorial statement of *The New York Times,* commenting on his premature retirement.

"He retired with honor and dignity. . . . He will be long remembered as a great player and a great human being."

Warren Spahn

Warren Spahn

Warren Spahn was the "Iron Man" of modern baseball. In the course of a storied career that spanned twenty-one years of major league pitching, he set a number of endurance records, and his 363 victories still stands as a National League record for left-handers.

Baseball for Spahn was a chosen career as far back as his knee pants days, as far back as the days of the Great Depression of the 1930's, when he was scampering over the Buffalo sandlots playing with a makeshift bat and ball.

His father, Ed Spahn, had been in his young days a fine semipro player, and it was his fondest wish that his son go on to the very top—to the major leagues.

With his father's help, and his inspiration, Warren became an outstanding player in the organized sandlot leagues around Buffalo, and then with the Casenovia Post team of the American Legion league.

He was a first baseman then, and a fine one. However, when he entered South Park High School and tried out for the team, he was told frankly that he stood little chance. The team had an all-scholastic first baseman, and no newcomer would win that job.

Hopefully, then, Warren volunteered the information that he also could pitch. In truth, he had done very little pitching on the sandlots. But his father had taught him a bit about throwing curves, and in long afternoon sessions in their yard, father and son had worked out with ball and mitt. The practice had given him a certain amount of control and poise. At least the pitcher's mound wasn't a complete stranger to him.

Perhaps as much to his own surprise as to the surprise of the high school coach, his tryout as a pitcher was an absolute sensation. He made the team.

By the time his junior year arrived, Warren was the high school marvel of Buffalo. He didn't lose a game, repeated the performance in his senior year, and capped the amazing season with a no-hitter.

Pitching like that is certain to grab the attention of the major league scouts. One in particular, Billy Myers, a scout for the Boston Braves, camped on his trail in the spring of 1940, Warren's senior year. Myers in fact had made a special stakeout of the Buffalo area, scouting it for years and gaining a reputation as an honest scout who considered the welfare of the young players he signed as well as the club he worked for.

When he approached Warren, then, in the spring of 1940, his credentials were impeccable. It was against the rules to sign a youngster who was still in school, however. Myers simply entered into general preliminary discussions with Warren and his father. What he said apparently made good sense. When the young hurler graduated from South Park High, he was formally signed, and was sent to the Braves' farm team at Bradford, Pennsylvania.

Bradford was not one of the better-hitting teams in the Pony League, and Warren suffered for it. In his first twelve games he compiled an earned run average of 2.73, a quite creditable mark, and deserving of better than the 5–4 record he earned for it. Then, late that summer, experimenting with a new delivery for an overhand curve, the youngster tore tendons in his left arm. He was through for the season.

If Bradford wasn't much of a team, its parent club the Boston Braves wasn't much better in its own league. A chronic second-division dweller, led by the droll figure of Casey Stengel, the Braves were in the position where they looked hopefully at all their young players, seeking in them the smallest kernel of potential stardom.

Thus, the fact that he had suffered a serious shoulder injury did not bar Warren from his chance in spring training the following season. The Braves gave him a fair shot —and he hit the bull's-eye.

Watching him pitch a two-hitter against the Boston regulars one afternoon, Stengel cocked his head to one side and studied the nineteen-year-old protégé carefully. Even then Warren had the graceful form, the smooth delivery that was to mark his style for so many years.

When he walked off the mound at the end of the game, he was watched with new respect by the Braves' pilot.

"If ever a kid looked like a pitcher, this fella's it," Casey remarked.

Promoted to Evansville, in the Three-I League, on the basis of his fine spring showing, Warren demonstrated his gratitude and his talent in the higher league by winning 19 and losing only 6, leading the league in victories, percentage and with his 1.83 ERA. Included were seven shutouts, three one-hitters, and a scoreless streak of forty-two consecutive innings.

The Braves were duly impressed. There were some men in the front office who thought the brilliant young hurler should be promoted to the big leagues in 1942. These executives felt that he was good enough—especially considering the team's general ineptitude. Furthermore, new young blood was needed to bolster the team's fading popularity with the impatient Boston fans.

Stengel was more conservative. On the field, and in his dealings with the press, he may have given the impression he was a clown, but not when it came to the hard facts of making a baseball decision. His public image indeed was one of an eccentric, but managing the Boston Braves in those fruitless years brought out the joker in Stengel. Mostly, it was the manifestation of his despair. It was a bad ball club.

His opinions regarding Spahn, therefore, had little to do with the Boston fans or any temporary improvement he might provide in the Braves. Casey was trying to rebuild the team with young talent. It was not a task completed in a hurry. Even talent needed time to mature.

That was Stengel's decision regarding Spahn. He told the disappointed young pitcher the facts during spring training, at a time when Warren felt he was headed directly for the Braves.

Rather than have him sit out the season on the bench, or take the chance on spoiling his style, perhaps reinjuring his shoulder trying to win for the hitless Braves, Stengel advised another season of minor league ball.

Disappointed—yes, but not despairing, Warren went to Hartford, in the Eastern League. There he showed Stengel he was ready any time he was needed by compiling a 1.96 ERA while winning 17 and losing 12.

Stengel was convinced. At the tail end of the 1942 season he brought Spahn to Boston. And then he was convinced he had been right in the first place to keep the youngster in the minors a while longer. In two starts, Warren was belted from the mound. Though escaping the burden of either loss, he did not show much evidence of big league pitching. In a total of four appearances, numbering 16 innings, he gave up 10 runs and 25 hits for a 5.63 ERA.

Stengel's faith might have been shaken, but it was not lost. He maintained that the time would shortly come when Spahn would prove his worth. He was looking forward to better things in 1943. But other parties had first call on Warren's services that winter. He was drafted into the United States Army.

Spahn was not one of those professional athletes fortunate to spend the war as a morale-builder for other servicemen. He served as a sergeant in a combat engineer battalion attached to the 9th Armored Division. He was involved in fierce fighting on the European front, was wounded in the foot, and was awarded a field commission as second lieutenant.

After V-E Day, he served in the occupation forces for nearly a year before being sent back to civilian life—and the Boston Braves.

Now under the management of Billy Southworth, the Braves were again rebuilding. During the war they had struggled along with a collection of youngsters and old-timers and a few players with ailments serious enough to keep them out of the services. Every team in baseball did the same—and now every team was rebuilding, welcoming home their war veterans, promoting young talent from the farms, hoping that years away from the diamond had not sapped the talents of men like Spahn.

By the time Warren shed his army uniform the 1946 season had begun. At the request of the Braves he reported to them almost at once. Instead of the usual weeks of spring training he worked out in pregame practice and in the bullpen, trying to sharpen the pitching skills that had lain dormant for nearly four years. It was a formidable task indeed.

Finally, he felt he was ready to pitch. However, Southworth didn't want to rush him. After all, the pilot mused, Spahn had little major league experience, and in fact had not thrown a ball in a professional game since 1942.

The Braves' skipper waited for an easy moment to give Warren his second debut as a major league pitcher. One night in Boston, with the Braves losing, 8–0, in the seventh inning, he gave him the call out of the bullpen.

Spahn responded as though he had never been away. He retired all nine men he faced without allowing so much as a hard-hit ball.

Impressed, but still cautious, Southworth eased him back to competition gradually with several more relief jobs. Then he put him into the starting rotation. Warren lost his first major league game soon afterward, to the Giants, but then won five straight. He finished the 1946 season with an 8–5 record and a 2.93 ERA.

The Braves were satisfied. It was a fine comeback performance after four years in the army. They expected even a better one in 1947—and years of star quality pitching from their young left-hander.

They got it.

He began the 1947 season as though he intended never to be beaten. He won eight straight games, then lost the ninth on a bad play by one of his outfielders. Exhibiting a good fast ball, a terrific curve, a newly developed change-up, and, above all, pinpoint control, Spahn became the sensation of the league. He was the stopper of the club, the pitcher Southworth counted on to win the big ones.

At the same time the other clubs, awakened to his talents, saved their own best pitchers to face him. As a result he was continually locked in fierce mound struggles. Many of his wins were narrow decisions. Many of his losses were the results of inadequate hitting or bad breaks.

With two weeks to go in the season, he was 17–10. He wanted to win 20 in this, his first full season in major league uniform. He did it, and he did it in fantastic style, by pitching three straight shutouts and a 2–1 game in his final four starts.

Third baseman Bob Elliott won the MVP in the National League that season, for his outstanding hitting and fielding, enabling the Braves to finish third. However, Spahn was certainly the league's most valuable pitcher. In winning 21 games, he led the league with 290 innings pitched, a 2.33 earned run average and seven shutouts.

His victory total would have been even higher with some hitting support. In the ten games he lost, the Braves scored a total of eleven runs, and were shut out five times.

Warren's explosive emergence as one of the best pitchers in baseball aroused a good deal of speculation around the league. What did this comparative newcomer have that made him so effective?

"A terrific fast ball," said Pee Wee Reese, star shortstop of the Dodgers.

"He's got a great overhand curve," said Ben Chapman, manager of the Phillies.

Spahn's own receiver, however, pinpointed his unique talent, the one item in his repertoire that made him a superstar, that would be his hallmark as he wrote his name indelibly in the pages of baseball history.

"Control, that's Spahn's secret," Phil Masi said. "That guy knows where every pitch is going."

For seventeen years that uncanny control, that ability to consistently exploit a batter's weakness, to shave the strike zone as though with a razor, made Warren Spahn one of the great pitchers. Until the closing moments of his long career, when more than two decades on the mound finally took their toll of that magical left arm, he was up there with the best every year. From 1947, his first full season with the Braves, until 1963, he was a 20-game winner 13 times, an all-time major league record for a left-hander. Only Christy Mathewson, a right-hander, ever won 20 in as many seasons; only Cy Young ever won 20 more times—16.

Starting with that first full year, he was held to less than 20 wins in but four of his complete seasons thereafter.

In 1962, after six straight seasons of 20 or more victories, he was held to an 18–14 mark. With a little hitting help that could just as well have been 22–10. Three times he was beaten 2–1 and once 2–0.

One of his biggest seasons was the 1957 campaign, some years after the Braves had moved to Milwaukee.

A year before they had been nosed out for the pennant by the Cardinals. Now they felt the time was ripe for their first flag since 1948. In spring training manager Fred Haney worked them to exhaustion. He felt that his men had lost too many close ball games in 1956, had allowed complacency and overconfidence to steal the pennant from their grasp at the last moment. He wanted no repetition of past mistakes.

Under his whiplash command and their own renewed vigor, they dashed out to a quick lead when the season began. Spahn won the opening game and set the pace. The Braves won nine of their first ten games. Moreover, their manner of winning was impressive, reflective of their new attitude. Five of those nine victories were by one-run margins; their only loss was in ten innings, by one run. Four times they had to come from behind to win. They were playing smart, aggressive baseball, taking advantage of every break, every error, while giving away nothing in return.

They played like champions. There was Joe Adcock

on first base, Danny O'Connell at second, Johnny Logan at shortstop, Ed Mathews on third. Bill Bruton was in center field, flanked by Bobby Thomson and Hank Aaron. Spahn led a pitching staff that also starred Lew Burdette, Bob Buhl, Gene Conley and Ernie Johnson. Del Crandall was their catcher.

Spahn was thirty-six years old, pitching like a youngster of twenty-one.

The Braves by no means ran away from the league. Despite their fast start, they had the Cardinals, Reds and Dodgers hard on their heels. In the early going there was seldom more than four or five games separating the entire first division.

On June 15, the Braves executed a trade that virtually wrapped up the pennant for them. They obtained Red Schoendienst from the Giants, giving up Thomson, O'Connell and pitcher Ray Crone. A thirty-four-year-old second baseman who was the league's All-Star selection eight times, Schoendienst gave the infield the extra strength it needed. He was also known as one of baseball's toughest hitters in the clutch.

On the first of September the Braves rode a seven-game lead. Spahn pitched his seventeenth victory that day, and his seventh in a row. Three days later he beat the Cubs, 8–0, with the forty-first shutout of his career, a new National League record for left-handers. (He extended that number to 63 shutouts before retiring.)

His nineteenth win was a 7–2 victory. Then twice he was stopped in his quest for number 20 before beating the Cubs again. He won one more before the Braves nailed down the pennant. He was top man in the league.

Not content now merely with bringing Milwaukee its first flag, Spahn and the Braves wanted to beat the Yankees in the World Series.

The struggle was a grueling one. Spahn was once more the victim of bad luck and weak stickwork. He lost the opener, 3–1. Burdette evened the count with a 4–2 victory next day, but when the Yankees routed four pitchers in a 12–3 debacle in the third game, most observers thought the Braves were finished.

Warren got his second chance in the fourth game. The Yankees clipped him for a run in the first frame, but then he bore down, retired eleven men in a row before Gerry Coleman singled in the fifth. By then the Braves had slammed home four runs on homers by Aaron and Frank Torre.

Spahn had a 4–1, six-hitter going when the Yankees came up in the ninth. Continuing in fine style, he retired Hank Bauer and Mickey Mantle. The fans rose and headed for the exits.

Then Yogi Berra and Gil McDougald singled, and the fans stopped, hesitated, and sat down again. Elston Howard, stepping in to hit, was the tying run. The game wasn't over yet.

Manager Haney walked out to the mound. Milwaukee fans screamed at him to keep Spahn in the game. But he was just checking on the pitching strategy for Howard, and, further, giving his pitcher a few extra moments to steady himself.

Spahn worked the count to three-and-two on Howard. Then, in one of the rare lapses of his lifetime, he fed the Yankee catcher an inside pitch that was blasted out of the ball park for a home run. The game was tied.

He retired Andy Carey to end the inning. Few, however, thought he would pitch the tenth inning. It was apparent that he had tired. Two good relief men were in the bullpen. But Haney stayed with him. Perhaps he felt that in any case his best pitcher was Spahn, and he would win or lose with him. Perhaps, too, in a moment of empathy—though he was as hard as nails—he knew how much Spahn wanted to win this contest himself now, to redeem, in a way, a debt he had incurred with one pitch.

Certainly Haney knew that in these circumstances a pitcher with the courage of Warren Spahn would muster every ounce of strength, every atom of skill at his command. That was worth more than a fresh pitcher from the bullpen. Or so he hoped.

His decision soon looked like the wrong one, although again a bit of bad luck was involved. Warren retired the first two batters in the tenth. Then he fooled Tony Kubek with a pitch, but the speedy infielder turned his slow roller into a base hit. Hank Bauer followed with a triple, and the Yankees led, 5–4.

With heavy heart and sagging shoulders Spahn got Mantle on a fly ball for the third out, and walked slowly back to the dugout. It appeared certain that he was headed for his second defeat of the Series.

Nippy Jones pinch-hit for him to start the bottom of the tenth, and was hit on the foot by the first pitch. Felix Mantilla ran for him. Schoendienst sacrificed. Then Johnny Logan ripped a double down the left field line, scoring Mantilla with the tying run. Again the score was tied. The Braves, and Spahn, were not beaten yet.

Ed Mathews stepped in. County Stadium was a bedlam of noise as the huge crowd begged the star slugger to connect with one.

Yankee relief pitcher Bob Grim toiled carefully. Mathews fouled off the first two pitches. Ahead now, Grim tried to get him to bite at a bad pitch. Mathews waited. The count went to two-and-two. Grim came in with the next pitch over the plate. Mathews swung. A great roar went up with the crack of the bat. No question about that drive—it rocketed over the right field fence for the game-winning homer!

The World Series was far from finished. The Yankees were not the sort to roll over and play dead. But after that exciting finish the rest of the Series seemed almost anticlimactic. Burdette won his second game of the Series, 1–0; then the Yankees evened the Classic at three-all with a 3–2 victory.

It was Spahn's turn again. To his chagrin, however, he was in bed with the flu. Burdette, pitching with one day's rest, replaced him, and won his third contest with a 5–0 shutout.

The Braves had their World's Championship.

Warren Spahn won baseball's highest pitching honor in that memorable season of 1957—the Cy Young Award.

At his age, it seemed an appropriate encomium, akin to formal recognition on the occasion of his imminent retirement, as the best pitcher in baseball, and one of the best ever.

Only Warren Spahn had no intention of retiring. Not even soon. Maybe he *was* thirty-six, and maybe many baseball experts reckoned he could call it a career, bow out with honor—but he was far from ready to quit.

There were indeed many who predicted he could not repeat in 1958, not at his age and with his years of labor. There were some who thought he should quit when he was a winner, become a coach. A few experts thought he might have another fair year or two left in the old arm.

Hardly anybody expected him to go on to even greater glory, to bigger years, to more remarkable pitching performances.

That is precisely what he did. It was almost as though at thirty-six, when he could reasonably have been considered in the twilight of his career, he began a new one instead.

He won 22 games in 1958, leading the Braves to another pennant. In the World Series he won two more games, losing one, while the Yankees were regaining their championship.

He went on to three successive years of 21 victories each before being stopped, as mentioned earlier, with 18 wins, hampered by weak hitting. This, of course, was a problem he faced throughout the major part of his career. In recounting the fact that he won 20 or more games for 14 seasons, it must be taken into account, to realize the entire picture, that he was on a pennant winner only three times; half the time the Braves finished fourth or lower.

In 1960, now thirty-nine years old, he pitched the first no-hitter of his career. A truly amazing performance at that age. And the next year he did it again!

Each season the fans, the writers, his teammates and the men who had to hit against him awaited the inevitable moment when that fabulous control would waver, the curve would flatten out. And each year he confounded them all.

He was forty-two years old when he won 23 and lost 7 for the Braves, matching the highwater mark of his career reached exactly ten years earlier.

And then, when it appeared that somehow time had been conquered by Warren Spahn, that inevitable moment won out—as it must.

He just didn't have it any more in 1964. He lost it all, save for those fleeting moments during the course of a game when for a few pitches, perhaps for a few innings, the flash of the old magic was there.

He won 6 and lost 13.

The Braves sold him to the Mets that winter. And in

midseason of 1965 the Mets dealt him to the Giants. They in turn gave Spahn his release at the end of the season. Between both clubs he won 7 and lost 16.

After twenty-one years, it was time to leave the mound.

The record books tell the story of Warren Spahn's career. It is a story that will in time be etched in a bronze plaque, to hang on the wall in the Hall of Fame, where Warren Spahn belongs.

Heroes of Today

Don Drysdale ••••••••••••••••••••••••••••••••••••••

Don Drysdale

Don Drysdale stood on the mound in Connie Mack Stadium, his handsome young face impassive, awaiting patiently the umpire's call to begin the duel. The shouts and the murmurs of the crowd fell upon his ears in a soft wave of sound, like the roar of surf heard from a distance. For the briefest moment young Don felt outside himself, like one of those people in the grandstand, looking down upon the floodlit playing field, the brown apron of the infield neatly ironed, the green turf gleaming emerald in the glare of the powerful lights. The grass was newly cut and smelled of spring. The blackness of the night, even blacker against the false white light of the ball park, hid the smokestacks and the factory buildings and the oil refineries just across the river.

In Connie Mack Stadium only the world of baseball existed.

For Don Drysdale it had always been so. He had dreamed the dream common to so many boys. Now he was among those fortunate few to whom the dream becomes reality.

He focused all his attention now on that reality, as Richie Ashburn dug in at the plate to be the Phillies' leadoff batter. And Don Drysdale, nineteen years old, prepared to throw the first ball of his first starting assignment in the uniform of the Brooklyn Dodgers.

His teammates had given him a run to work with in the top half of the first inning. That helped to calm his nervousness. He did not lack for confidence, but realized the limits of his experience—a season and a half of minor league ball and a one-inning relief appearance just a week earlier against these same Phillies. It wasn't very much to go on for a major league starting pitcher. Don knew he was on trial.

He had another moment, before throwing the first ball, to ponder on the wonder of it all. There was the great Roy Campanella in a crouch, wagging his fingers at him. Campy had been playing pro ball in the Negro Leagues before Don had been born. And Murry Dickson, the Phillies' hurler, was thirty-nine—old enough to be his father!

Then there was no more time for reflection. Ashburn was waving his bat, waiting.

Don wound up and threw a curve over the outside corner. Ashburn swung and missed. The fleet Philadelphia outfielder stepped out of the batter's box a moment and looked out at the mound appraisingly. That had been a neat curve for a kid pitcher. Ashburn stepped back in, took a ball high, then swung and missed at another curve. Then a fast ball zipped over the corner. Ashburn swung and missed for strike three!

Bobby Morgan stepped up. In his inning of relief work Don had walked Morgan. This time he struck him out. Next came Granny Hamner. Don struck him out, too.

Three straight strikeouts to launch his first major league start!

His second inning was less impressive. The leadoff batter stroked a single to left on his first pitch. Angry at himself, Don kicked at the rubber. He pitched too quickly to the second man and walked him.

Campanella trotted out to the mound. "Hey, man, slow it down," the catcher cautioned. "Let the hitter wait. He ain't goin' nowhere until you throw."

Don nodded, but it is likely he didn't quite hear. He was overanxious now. Impatient, too, perhaps a fault that was to haunt him for many seasons to come.

He got the next batter on a foul pop, then struck out Andy Seminick. But an infield hit loaded the bases.

Dickson, the pitcher, stepped in to hit.

Campanella, Jackie Robinson and Gil Hodges formed a council at the mound. The veteran Dodger stars cautioned the young hurler against losing Dickson. He was only the pitcher, but he held a bat in his hands, and that made any hitter dangerous. It wouldn't do to let up on him. At the same time, Don was warned not to press so hard that he threw the ball away.

Don blew out his breath and indicated he was ready. The men went back to their positions. Campanella squatted behind the plate and hung out the sign for a curve.

Don came down with the pitch, a tangle of arms and legs and flapping elbows. The curve was a good one; Dickson swung and lifted a pop fly behind the infield. Reese backpedaled for it furiously. Snider raced in from center field. With two out, the runners were flying around the bases.

It was a tough chance. The ball didn't have much height and was dropping fast.

Helplessly Don stood on the mound and watched its descent, hoping somebody would get there. Reese had the best angle on it. The Dodger captain called Snider off, put on an extra burst of speed, lunged and caught the ball off his shoetops on the dead run.

Don walked off the mound wiping the perspiration from his brow.

The crisis, coming so early in the game, served to chase the remaining few butterflies from the young pitcher's stomach. He had weathered the rough seas. Now he could sail ahead.

Inning by inning thereafter he mowed down the

Philly hitters. Though they touched him for seven more singles the rest of the way, he was never in serious trouble again. He struck out nine, and allowed a run in the eighth only after his teammates had given him a 6–0 cushion to relax upon.

When he struck out Glen Gorbous to record the first victory of his brief major league existence, Don would have been forgiven a leap of joy. As it was, he simply grinned, turned to accept the handshake from Robinson and the pat from Reese, and walked calmly off the mound as though winning and striking out nine were an old story to him.

In his heart was undoubtedly the wish that someday this would indeed be the case. Certainly he had worked hard and with intense purpose toward that day. Almost since he could remember wanting anything at all, he had wanted to be a professional baseball player.

The verdant garden of Southern California is indeed a paradise for growing boys interested in sports. The brilliant sunshine and seemingly endless atmosphere of summer give extra impetus to physical activity. The parks are always green and the flowers forever blossom. Football is played when the calendar calls for the season, but baseball can be played twelve months of the year.

This was where Donald Scott Drysdale was born and brought up, in Van Nuys, a pleasant suburb of Los Angeles. This was where his early zeal for baseball developed, nurtured carefully by his father. Scott Drysdale had been a better than fair semiprofessional baseball player in his youth. He wanted better for his son. He wanted the best, in fact. He wanted his son to be a major league pitcher, and he was determined to give him every chance to make the grade.

Serious pitching when a boy is still growing can affect the arm, so that professional pitching later is often impossible. With this knowledge in mind, Scott Drysdale trained his son to be a sandlot second baseman.

There the boy remained, a young star of the keystone sack, playing for the Van Nuys Post in American Legion ball, a team coached by his own father. He was a star, too, at Van Nuys High School, not only in baseball but in football. This versatility almost proved his undoing. Playing quarterback for Van Nuys—pitching a football, at least—he suffered a shoulder injury that threatened to end all thoughts of a professional baseball pitching career.

However, a winter of rest and diathermy treatment healed damaged ligaments. Despite the narrow escape, Don did not stop playing football. He knew the risk he was taking, but refused to play it safe by resigning from the high school football team. He loved football almost as much as he loved baseball. He liked the action, the body contact, the take-charge feeling of running the team that good quarterbacks possess. And he knew he was needed. He wouldn't let his coach and his teammates down.

As a result, he suffered another shoulder injury in his senior year. The damage was minor, but the two injuries were to play an important role in his baseball future.

By now, just past his sixteenth birthday, he was six feet tall, handsome and muscular. His father felt he was ready to begin pitching. For years they had talked about it, and Don had practiced pitching in odd moments. Then the day came, in the course of an American Legion game, when Scott Drysdale took his son off second base, gave him the ball, and told him he was the relief pitcher.

Neither father nor son knew that by wonderful coincidence, a Brooklyn Dodger scout named Goldie Holt was watching the game, looking around for promising youngsters. What he saw of Don Drysdale's relief performance made him hunch forward on his seat in fascinated interest. The boy had nothing but speed, a sidearm right-hand whiplike speed that had the batters striking out, popping up, or grounding weakly to the infield.

Coming on in the fourth inning, Don swept through the North Hollywood Post lineup like a whirlwind. He shut them out the rest of the way, giving up two singles.

Goldie Holt was sufficiently impressed to stay around after the game. He introduced himself to Mr. Drysdale and Don. Of course, since Don was still in high school he was not allowed to make any actual overtures, but he invited the youngster to join a Saturday amateur league that was being organized by the Dodgers.

That invitation was enough to whet Don's appetite. The fact that the Dodger scout had bothered to talk to him meant he had seen something there to interest him. It was a small first step. But a definite one.

Now Don was a pitcher. He hurled for the Van Nuys Post and for his high school team. He began learning now in earnest. He needed to learn control, to develop an efficient, comfortable style that would not overstrain his arm, and he needed to develop a curve.

With the help of his father and additional help from his high school coach, Don broadened his skills. He became the best pitcher in American Legion ball, then in the Dodgers-sponsored amateur league, and in high school. Just before graduation in June of 1954 he pitched the winning game that gave Van Nuys the high school league championship.

Now Don had ample reason to be pleased with himself. Furthermore, he had good reason to believe that the major league scouts would be zeroing in on him, the Dodgers' Goldie Holt in the forefront. But nothing happened. A few offers came from West Coast universities offering athletic scholarships. Nothing more. Don didn't want college. At least, not then. He did have thoughts about attending college in between baseball seasons, as some professionals did. But first he wanted that status as a professional ballplayer.

He was disappointed by the lack of action from the scouts. Neither he nor his father could fathom this lack of interest, considering Don's sparkling record as an amateur and Goldie Holt's initial encouraging response.

About two weeks after graduation Holt appeared. He unraveled the mystery for them by exposing to them his own reservations about Don's potential.

As Goldie Holt explained it, everybody was concerned about Don's right arm. Naturally, in the course of scouting him, the major league clubs had unearthed the fact that he had injured his arm in football. This threw his future worth into doubt. That he had the talent was apparent; the question was, could his injured arm withstand the strains of major league pitching? Arm injuries were funny; they might heal perfectly and disappear, only to reappear years later under the pressure of sustained work.

However, the scout went on, the Dodgers were still interested. He had been able to convince them that the risk from the injuries was small. Yet they felt some accounting had to be taken of this risk, no matter how minimal. They were willing to sign Don, but without a large bonus. And in any case, they felt he needed minor league experience, which would have been impossible under the "bonus rule." They would give him four thousand dollars to sign, therefore, and send him to Bakersfield.

Don and his father considered this offer for several days. Then they accepted. In the absence of a better deal, the Dodger offer was fair enough. Besides, it was a sound point that in the long run Don would fare better with some minor league experience than by sitting on the Dodger bench as a "bonus baby."

That point was proven at Bakersfield. All fire and fast ball, he won eight while losing five. He impressed his manager there with his determination and his spirit, but his overall performance was inconclusive. It was good, but not spectacular. He needed more work, especially on his curve. He needed to improve his pacing, to learn how to mix his speeds.

When he reported at Vero Beach for spring training the following year, he was considered nothing more than one of the many promising youngsters in the farm system. They were there by the dozens, working out with big leaguers, taking part in "B" squad games, and on occasion getting a chance for an inning or two in an exhibition game.

Don got such a chance one day, against the Yankees. The Dodgers were losing, 8–2, in the seventh inning. This seemed like a reasonable spot to throw in a young pitcher. Manager Walt Alston sent in the eighteen-year-old right-hander from Bakersfield to see what he could do.

Mickey Mantle was Don's first batter. Alston couldn't have found a tougher man for a young pitcher to face in his first action against a major league team—even in an exhibition game.

Don got him out on a pop fly to first. Then he retired Bill Skowron on a ground ball. Elston Howard skied to Snider.

One inning was all Walt Alston cared to have Don work so early in the season. He wanted to give other young pitchers a chance as well. But that one inning won Don special attention. He was no longer just one of the crowd. The Dodger coaches took pains to work with him. He was given more exhibition innings to pitch. Even the blasé New York sportswriters took notice of the big right-hander with the sidearm fast ball.

At the end of the training season Don was promoted to Montreal, a tremendous jump in classification. Montreal was just one step away from the big leagues.

Armed with an improved curve ball, encouraged by his rapid advancement, Don set to work at Montreal with increased vigor and determination.

Soon after the 1955 season began Greg Mulleavy, the Montreal manager, sent a glowing report to the Dodgers. "The boy's a tiger," he said. "He's got the hitters backing away from that sweeping fast ball of his. Tremendous competitive spirit. His only fault, if he has one, is getting so mad at himself he forgets to think. Needs slowing down regularly by his catcher."

Just before midseason Don had seven wins and two defeats. Then he won his eighth, shutting out Toronto. After the game, in the clubhouse, he went over to a big metal case in the corner for a soft drink. As he stood against it, left hand holding the bottle, right hand resting on the edge, the lid fell, slamming down hard on his right hand.

The pain was excruciating. The fingers began to swell at once. Despite the agony, Don looked swiftly around the room, checking to see if anyone had noticed.

But he was alone in the corner. Quickly he plunged his hand into the icy waters of the case. For a moment it soothed the pain. He held the hand there for a moment, then walked back to his locker and dressed, slowly and carefully, lest he emit a wince of pain that a teammate might notice.

Don was caught in a dilemma. The most obvious thing to do, of course, was report the accident to the team doctor. He was reluctant to do that, however. The season was going so well, he was sure that the Dodgers would bring him up either later in the year or at the latest the following year. To be sidelined now could stall that advancement, perhaps for another whole season. Worse yet, there was the barest possibility that the accident might remind the Dodgers of his football injuries. They might mark him as one of those athletes, injury-prone, who spend their entire careers almost, but not quite, fulfilling their earlier promise.

He decided therefore to keep pitching, to tell no one of the accident. The hand felt stiff, but by soaking it in ice whenever he had a moment's privacy he kept the swelling to a minimum. When his next pitching turn came, however, he knew he needed desperate measures. Even gripping a ball would cause him crippling pain. In the clubhouse before game time, therefore, when nobody was watching, he sprayed his hand with ethyl chloride, a freezing compound used by the trainers as a pain killer.

Incredibly, he managed six good innings against Buffalo, holding a 4–1 lead, before the effects of the anesthetic began to wear off. All he could do then was palm the ball and throw it. He was knocked out of the box. Relief pitching saved his ninth win, but Don knew that further troubles awaited him.

Such was his youthful pride and determination, his

courage and his raw talent, that he continued to pitch under the effects of the ethyl chloride. He must have had doubts about the wisdom of this. It must have occurred to him that he might be ruining his pitching career, damaging the hand for all time. At the same time, with an understandable rationalization, he perhaps believed that eventually the bruised hand would heal itself perfectly, and that pitching even under such a handicap was better than sitting on the bench.

He began losing steadily. Even this did not deter him. Partly this was because many of his losses were marginal affairs, 2–1, 3–2 ball games; Montreal was not hitting behind him. Four times they failed to get him a run. Then, too, in the early innings he pitched well; only when the effects of the pain-killer wore off did enemy batters begin to pummel him.

Under the circumstances of the general Montreal slump and Don's early-inning effectiveness, manager Mulleavy suspected nothing. And so Don went on, pitching with a right hand doused in an anesthetic, until the last week of the season. Only then did he believe it safe to show the injury to the team doctor. Of course, that finished his pitching chores for the season. He was in fact warned not to throw the ball again for at least a month. A carefully prescribed regimen of treatment and exercise was prepared for him. He was told he was lucky to have escaped without permanent damage.

Back home in California, a much-chastened Don Drysdale now worried about his future. After his injury he had won three and lost nine, giving him an 11–11 record—not much of a recommendation for promotion to the Dodgers.

However, for once he was in luck. When he reported to Vero Beach the following spring, the hand completely healed, he found that the Dodgers were short of pitchers. Moreover, many of the Dodger stars were veterans in their declining years. It was an old team. It needed young players. Manager Alston was willing to overlook the raw statistics of Don's Montreal record in favor of his obvious potential. But the youngster would have to prove in spring training that his hand would give no trouble, and that he could pitch consistently good ball.

Accordingly, Don was given the full treatment. He was worked hard, made to throw batting practice, to the coaches, and finally sent regularly into exhibition games against the toughest major league teams. And he passed every test. He was ready. Just before opening day of the 1956 season, manager Alston announced that Don was being promoted to the Dodgers.

He beat Philadelphia in that memorable initial starting assignment. Five days later the Pirates knocked him out of the box. Alston decided that the young fireballer was not quite ready for steady work. In the opening days of the season he needed him in the rotation, but on May 15 the Dodgers bought pitcher Sal Maglie from the Indians. This venerable hurler, long a scourge of the Dodgers when he pitched for the Giants, had been waived out of the league just a year earlier. He didn't make it in Cleveland, and the Dodgers bought him. Maglie made the big difference. He became Alston's fourth starter, enabling Don to be saved for spot pitching and relief assignments. Furthermore, the wily old veteran proved to be a valuable teacher. He took Don under his wing and taught him all the tricks that had won him the nickname of "The Barber" in the National League—the man who gave close shaves to both the batters and the plate.

Don won 5 and lost 5 in his first season, including

a key 3–1 victory over the Giants in the final week of the season. The win projected the Dodgers into first place, and helped sew up the pennant. He had a 2.64 earned-run average, and the Brooklyn baseball writers voted him Dodger Rookie of the Year.

Don wasn't all that happy about the 5–5 record. What was more important, however, was that Alston was satisfied. He felt that on the whole the youngster had shown tremendous promise. He had done most of what had been expected. He needed experience. The Dodgers expected much more from him in the future.

He began giving more the following year. While the aging veterans finally collapsed and most of the young players failed to deliver, Don came through. Without him the Dodgers wouldn't have even finished third. He won 17 and lost 9, and his 2.69 ERA tied him for second best in the league. With a little hitting, he would have won 20.

The Dodgers were delighted. "He's sweet and mean," said Roy Campanella, the great catcher. "A sweet pitcher and a mean competitor."

"Right now, I'd say Don is one of the most valuable pitchers in the game," Alston said. "He's a real fighter. Never in baseball have I seen a kid his age so unafraid of the hitters. He could become one of the great ones. I'm counting on him for twenty wins next year."

On the whole Alston's assessment of Don was accurate and prophetic. But there was many a pothole to fall into on Don's long road to baseball glory.

Too many things went wrong even before a ball was pitched to open the 1958 season. First, Don entered the Army for a six-month tour of duty right after the 1957 World Series. That meant he would miss almost all of spring training in 1958. Then Roy Campanella's car skidded on a patch of ice one January night, smashed into a pole, and left Roy in a wheelchair for life. The Hall of Fame catcher was an important instrument in Don's success thus far. Without him, Don would suffer. Campy's skill and encouragement and knowledge of hitters helped Don over the hurdles, and he had been able to curb the temper that at times threatened to blow the young pitcher right out of a ball game.

Finally, the Dodgers moved to Los Angeles. Their new home was the Coliseum. The park was a bad one. The left field stands stood only 250 feet from home plate, and were protected by a screen, 42 feet high, that the Dodgers soon dubbed "The Monster."

Handicapped by lack of spring training, Don began the 1958 season shakily, and discovered immediately that he had to abandon his best pitch—a fast ball on the fists—when the Dodgers were at home.

Hit off the thin part of the bat by a right-hand hitter, the ball usually went for an easy fly out to left field. In the Coliseum it either popped against the screen, or dropped over it for a home run. Pitching there became a nightmare for him. Similarly, the specter of The Monster haunted the other Dodger pitchers, and the hitters mistakenly altered their style trying to capitalize on the screen.

The Monster, the loss of Campanella, the natural attrition brought about by aging veterans, all hit the Dodgers at once. From pennant contenders they collapsed to seventh place. Not a regular hit .300. Johnny Podres was the team's big winner with 13 victories. Don won 12, but lost 13.

Reconciled to the Coliseum the following year, helped by trades and fresh young players, the Dodgers staged a dramatic comeback in 1959, and Don with them.

They won the pennant, he won 17 games against 13 defeats, led the league in strikeouts with 242 and won a World Series game as the Dodgers trounced the White Sox in six games.

Still Don was far from satisfied. He felt he could not be considered a truly successful pitcher until he won 20—and he was pessimistic about winning 20 at the Coliseum. Then further troubles assailed him. The once-great hitting attack of the Dodgers evaporated with the final failure of the players who had hallowed the grounds of Ebbets Field.

The old pros were either gone or going. Furillo had been released. Robinson was gone. Reese was gone. Hodges and Snider became part-time players. Campanella was gone.

The new Dodgers depended upon pitching, speed and craft. That wasn't always enough. Don began losing painfully close ball games. He lost a five-hitter to the Giants, 1-0, then a 2-1 game, then a 2-0 game. Several times, too, leading by such scores as 1-0, or 2-1, he was removed for a pinch hitter in the late innings as Alston strove to widen the lead. And then, having failed that, the Dodgers lost when the relief pitchers failed to hold the slim margins.

He was 15-14 in 1960 and 13-10 in 1961, but he was a much better pitcher than those records indicated. However, sunnier days lay ahead. In 1962 the Dodgers were moving to a newly-built stadium in Chavez Ravine.

"It's like starting all over again after four lost years," Don said to a sportswriter early in the 1962 campaign. Other Dodgers echoed his sentiments. Leaving the Coliseum had removed a burden from their backs—a real one as well as a psychological one.

Baseball history records that the Dodgers lost the pennant that year in a postseason playoff to the Giants. Largely that was due to a late-season injury that sidelined Sandy Koufax. Otherwise the Dodgers would have been unbeatable. The great Koufax and Don had teamed up earlier in the season to become one of the best pitching duets in baseball history. In one particular doubleheader in June, Koufax no-hit the Mets in the first game. Don came back in the second game with a three-hit, 3–1 win, striking out thirteen. It was his fourteenth victory, with three months still to go in the season. There was talk of his winning thirty games.

Truly now he had justified his complaints about the Coliseum. In Chavez Ravine he was demonstrating all the things that he had been promising for years. His sidearm fast ball worked like the crack of a whip. His curve fell precisely where he wanted.

Then came the injury to Koufax in July. Without him the burden of winning fell largely to Don. The strain began to tell. In August he beat the Cubs, 8–3, for his twentieth win, the first of many milestones in his career. Four days later, when he beat the Mets, it marked his one-hundredth win.

Adding to the strain now was a further key injury. Larry Sherry, the relief ace, hurt his arm and ankle and was lost. Then the heat of the tough pennant race began to tell on the younger Dodgers. They made mistakes, fumbled the ball, ran the bases foolishly. Friction developed. Alston and third-base coach Leo Durocher argued openly. The dissension hurt the club.

After his twenty-first victory, Don found it tough to win. After eleven straight wins, the Giants beat him, 5–4. He lost another tough one. In the final moments of the season, with the pennant hanging by a thread, he threw two straight shutouts. With three games left to play, the Dodgers needed just one victory to clinch the pennant.

They couldn't get the runs. The Cardinals beat them, 3-2. Then Don lost, 2-0, the Dodgers getting just two hits. And in the finale they were shut out again, 1-0. The season ended in a tie. Then they lost the playoffs to the Giants.

Looking for a ray of sunshine in the darkness of their unexpected defeat, the Dodgers found it in the emergence of Don Drysdale as the outstanding pitcher of the season in the major leagues. He led them all with his 25-9 record and 232 strikeouts.

In recognition, the Baseball Writers Association of America voted him the Cy Young Award, as the major leagues' "Pitcher of the Year."

All pitchers go through their careers losing well-pitched ball games. Some, of course, manage to compile fine records while spending their entire baseball lives with second-division teams. Few, however, can match the record of tough losses in which Don was involved. As the Dodgers' strong man—Koufax suffered chronically from injuries—Don pitched more games than anybody, and faced the best pitchers in the league. In 1963, when he won 19 and lost 17, the Dodgers scored only 35 runs for him in the course of those 17 losses!

He suffered similarly the following year, when he was 18-16. Not until 1965 did he win more than twenty again. That season, once again teaming up with Koufax, they pitched the Dodgers to a pennant. He won 23 and lost 12. While overshadowed by one of Sandy's most spectacular years, Don nevertheless was superb. Only Koufax could have beaten him out for the Cy Young Award.

Testimony to Don's importance that year are his

three key victories in the stretch run to the flag. The Giants were league-leaders then. First he beat the Braves, 3–1. Then he hurled the Dodgers into a first place tie with a 1–0 shutout of the Cardinals. Then his second straight shutout, a three-hitter, stopped the Braves again, 4–0. Two days later Koufax clinched the pennant, with a 3–1 victory.

The Dodgers' triumph and their subsequent World Series victory over the Twins (Don won one, lost one) was a miracle of pitching and running. Maury Wills, the shortstop, was the club's leading hitter with a .286 average—but he stole 94 bases. Between them, Don and Sandy won 49 games, slightly more than half of the 97 won by the Dodgers that season.

Identical 13–16 years followed that season. Such a record hardly seems to warrant Don's stature as one of the best pitchers in baseball. Nevertheless, the experts continued to rate him so. Never had they seen a pitcher perform so well and win so few. Typical was his 1–0 loss to Baltimore in the 1966 World Series, a four-hitter. The Dodgers suffered 17 shutouts that year, the worst record ever for a pennant winner. Only the Cardinals and the lowly Mets scored fewer runs for the season.

Typical, too, was the manner in which he came through with victories in the crucial, closing moments of the season. As the wire approached, with the Dodgers holding onto a slim lead over the Pirates and Giants, Don was superb—he won three straight, 6–1, 4–2 and 2–0, before losing, 4–3, to the Phillies.

Don had even tougher luck in 1967. Koufax retired and Wills was traded, leaving him with the brunt of the pitching burden, no hitting, and not even the inspired base-running of little Maury to help. The Dodgers collapsed like a deck of cards, finishing eighth. In the course of his 16 defeats, Don was supported by the incredible total of 15 runs! His ERA of 2.74 placed him ninth in the league.

The Dodgers weren't much of a team again in 1968, finishing seventh, and next to last in team batting average. Only the Mets were worse—and not by much.

Yet Don Drysdale, with a 14–12 record, practically assured himself a place in the Hall of Fame with a pitching performance that ranks in the "untouchable" class along with Joe DiMaggio's 56-game hitting streak and Maury Wills' 104 steals.

He began the season rockily, with only one win against three losses—the win a typical 1–0 Drysdale victory. Then he began to move. On May 14 he blanked the Cubs, 1–0, on two hits. Then he beat the Astros, 1–0, to balance his record at 3–3—every win a 1–0 victory.

A 2–0 win over the Cardinals made it three straight shutouts. Then he blanked the Astros, 5–0. The four straight shutouts, superb pitching though they indicated, still stood far from the records. Carl Hubbell owned the National League record of 46⅓ scoreless innings, Walter Johnson the major league record of 56 innings. Doc White held the record of most consecutive shutouts pitched, with five.

Now Don took dead aim at those marks.

Facing the Giants on May 31, he had a 3–0 lead going into the ninth, and 44 straight shutout innings.

He began the ninth by walking Willie McCovey. Then Jim Ray Hart singled. Dave Marshall walked to load the bases with nobody out. Twice before, during the streak, Don had faced loaded-bases situations in the ninth, but never with nobody out!

Dick Dietz was the batter for the Giants. Don went to two balls and two strikes—and then it looked as though his string had come to an end. An inside pitch hit Dietz on the left arm, forcing in a run.

Or did it?

At once plate umpire Harry Wendelstedt threw up his arms and called ball three. He ruled Dietz had made no effort to get away from the pitch, and had in fact moved his arm into the ball.

The call started an argument at home plate—but it held. Given the second chance and the few minutes rest, Don came back to get Dietz on a short fly to left. Ty Cline grounded into a force play at the plate, and Jack Hiatt popped to Wes Parker.

The crowd and the dugout exploded after the final out, mobbing and escorting Don back to the bench, pounding him on the back, shaking his hand.

He had five straight shutouts now, tying the major league record. He needed just two more shutout innings to beat Hubbell's league record in that department.

After the Giant squeaker, the next game was a breeze. He beat the Pirates, 5–0, for an unprecedented sixth straight shutout!

There are fascinating sidelight statistics that accompany that Hall of Fame streak. In the 54 shutout innings, Don fanned 42 and walked 9. The combined batting average of his opponents was .145. He gave up just 27 hits, only three of them for extra bases—all doubles.

Holder of the new National League record for successive shutout innings, Don went for Johnson's all-time record.

His opponents were the Phillies.

They didn't get a hit off Don in the first inning. They didn't get a hit in the second inning. Now Don was tied with the Big Train at 56 innings.

All he needed now was to retire the first batter in the third inning, and he would be the new record holder. Still exercising his mastery, he got his man, Roberto Pena, on a ground out. Then he completed the inning by striking out Larry Jackson and Cookie Rojas.

Then through the fourth inning, and still Don hadn't given up a hit, much less a run.

In the fifth, Tony Taylor and Clay Dalrymple led off with singles, Taylor going to third. Don struck out Pena, but pinch-hitter Howie Bedell flied out to left. Taylor scored. The breathtaking, incredible streak was over at 58⅔ innings.

It is a record likely never to be equaled.

Don left the game in the seventh during another Phillies rally. Hank Aguirre came on in relief to protect Don's eighth victory, a 5–3 affair.

Eight wins and three losses in June, yet only 14 and 12 at season's end, is a record testifying once again to Don Drysdale's history as a hard-luck pitcher. This time, it was more than just the ineffectiveness of the Dodgers. A shoulder injury in August further hampered him. He pitched with it for a while, but finally was forced to leave the rotation—only the third time in his career he ever missed even one turn!

He finished the 1968 season with a 2.15 ERA, sixth in the league. Thirty-two years old, he looked forward to several more years with the Dodgers, years he hoped would prove more fruitful to them, and to him. He had 204 lifetime victories, putting him into that 200-plus elite class among pitchers. Someday, when the blazing fast ball was gone and the curve hung, Don professed hopes of staying on as a coach, even a manager.

Certainly he had the talent and the wisdom for either of these two posts. And, with one of the all-time great pitching feats in baseball history behind him, he could look forward to his eventual place in the Hall of Fame.

Bob Gibson

Bob Gibson

If there was a time in the life of Bob "Hoot" Gibson that he could finger as the turning point, it might well be that evening in July, 1961, before a game with the Los Angeles Dodgers. That night Johnny Keane took over the managerial reins of the Cardinals as Solly Hemus was kicked out. As the Redbird players milled around the locker room before the game, getting into their uniforms, the new skipper walked over to Gibson's locker, stuck a baseball in his hands and said to him, "Here, you pitch tonight."

Gibson went out and beat the Dodgers, helping himself with a home run.

Such an incident smacks of the drama relegated to sports fiction. But in the world of sports, art often imitates life, and not vice versa. There are dramatic moments and heroic achievements in sports more sensational than anything written in the so-called Frank Merriwell style of sports fiction. Let us go back just a bit in the life of Bob Gibson, for example.

A month before Bob was born, in a black ghetto in Omaha, Nebraska, his father died. That left the family support to his mother and eldest brother, Josh, who was only fifteen at the time. There were seven children, and Mrs. Gibson spent long hours working in a laundry and as a cleaning woman to feed and clothe and house them. Josh helped, as did all the older children who could earn any money at all. Josh was big brother and father in the family.

When he was still a tot, Bob fell seriously ill with pneumonia, the disease that killed his father. As he lay in the hospital, big brother Josh came to him and promised him a bat and ball if he would get well. Bob recovered. He fell victim after that to a variety of other ailments, all of which might be blamed directly or indirectly on his ghetto life. He suffered from rickets, asthma, hay fever and a rheumatic heart.

But as soon as he was able to, he put the bat and the ball to good use, and he has been doing so to excellent purpose ever since.

Under the close care of Josh, Bob spent most of his free time after school playing at some sport. Josh worked at setting up YMCA sports leagues and for the Omaha recreation department. He made Bob try just a little bit harder, because he expected more from him, and wanted him to be a successful person at whatever it was he chose to do. It was Josh's theory that a youngster who learns to excel at sports, to adapt to its disciplines, is building a background, a basis, for his entire future.

As he grew into his teens, Bob overthrew his early disabilities and developed into a sturdy young man. Some of the allergies remained with him (and still affect him, today), but he learned to control them. At Omaha Technical High he became a three-letter man, playing basketball and baseball and high-jumping at track.

The Cardinals had their eye on him even then. When he graduated, they offered him a contract. Bob was ready to jump, but big brother Josh held him back.

"You're going to college," he said to Bob.

Creighton University in Omaha gave Bob a scholarship. There, studying philosophy (Creighton is a Jesuit school) he became a crack basketball player, and both star pitcher and slugging outfielder. He didn't get to finish, however.

In his senior year Josh took him to meet Bill Bergesch, who was general manager of the Cardinals' Omaha farm team. Josh and Bill had known each other for years; Bergesch had been supplying the city recreation department, where Josh worked, with baseball equipment.

Bob worked out on the mound for Bergesch and field manager Johnny Keane—and a Cardinals star was born.

Bob got into ten games for Omaha that summer, winning two and losing one. He didn't have much more than a good fast ball and a slider that didn't work more often than it did. Still, Keane liked what he saw, a factor that was to play its part in Bob's rebirth that fateful night in July, 1961.

Before the season was over, Keane sent him on to Columbus, in the Class A Sally League. There he was 4–3. The following year, 1958, he split the season between Omaha and Rochester. His combined record of 8–9 was not impressive, but his 2.45 earned run average at Rochester indicated that there was more to Gibson than his won-and-lost record.

He split the next seasons between Omaha and Rochester and brief appearances up at the big club, in St. Louis. The way he began with the Cardinals it appeared as though he would stay—and become an instant star. He beat the Reds and Jim O'Toole, 1–0, in his first major league start, July 30, 1959.

He didn't get to pitch much, however, and finished 3–5. In 1960 it was a similar story. He started at Rochester, was called up, but pitched intermittently, finishing 3–6.

Bob made no secret of the fact that he blamed his poor showing on lack of work. He blamed that on Solly Hemus, the Cardinals' manager. He made no secret of that, either. He and Hemus didn't get along.

That's where matters stood in Bob's career until July,

1961. Then Keane took over—and gave Bob the ball.

The reversal of form was gradual, but definite. Working regularly, Bob zoomed to 13–12 by the end of his first full season. His 3.24 ERA was fifth best in the league and best by a right-hander. The following year he was 15–13, which would have undoubtedly been improved upon had he not broken his leg toward the end of the season. His earned run average, down to 2.85, was again fifth best in the league.

There were whispers around the league about Bob in those early years. Some said that if you stayed close to Gibson for seven innings, you'd beat him. He wasn't a finisher. The implication was that Bob lacked a certain amount of courage, that in clutch situations he faltered—and then could be belted out.

The story was true only insofar as it was a fact that Bob did lose many a close contest—and in the final innings of a game. However, it was hardly due to lack of staying ability or courage. In fact, many of the close losses were not his fault at all.

The trouble was, Bob did not pace himself. From the first pitch of the game he gave it everything he had. Thus, by the seventh inning of the game, unless he had a lead big enough to coast on, he had to continue to deliver the maximum. Sometimes he didn't have any more to give by then; particularly was this so in midsummer, when the heat would wilt him. His records indicated that he pitched better in cooler weather.

Such a pitching technique is not a grievous fault. The great Whitey Ford pitched exactly that way for years. The difference was that Ford benefited from such back-up relief men as Luis Arroyo and Pedro Ramos. Gibson had no such fabulous firemen behind him. When he left a ball game in the latter stages with either a marginal lead or a marginal deficit, he stood little chance of coming home a winner.

Not until 1963, when the Cardinals made the big jump from sixth place to second, did Bob get support. When he did, his record jumped as well, to 18–9. That year, too, Bob drove in 20 runs, more than any of the league's *combined* pitching staffs.

When the Cardinals won the pennant in 1964, their first in almost twenty years, it was Hoot who won the deciding game, coming in to give a sterling relief performance. It was his 19th victory against 12 defeats. He would have had his 20, but for an umpire's decision. In August, when he had a 10–10 record, he was leading the Phillies, 7–1, in the fourth inning, when he allegedly threw his bat at pitcher Jack Baldschun. Hoot said the bat slipped, but the plate umpire thought otherwise and ejected him from the game. The Cardinals won, but since he hadn't pitched the required four and a half innings Gibson couldn't get credit for the win. He lost just two more games the rest of the year, one of those a 1–0 loss to the Mets in his last start.

The World Series with the Yankees was a dramatic one. Gibson won one and lost one as the teams split the first six contests. Then, for the money game, Keane chose Bob to start for the third time, against Mel Stottlemyre for the Yankees.

With his teammates giving him a 6–0 lead, Gibson coasted brilliantly until the sixth, when Mantle caught one of his fast balls for a three-run homer. Ken Boyer got one of the runs back with a home run, and Bob had a 7–3 lead going into the ninth.

Keane knew Gibson was tired. But he knew that at that precise moment Gibson was also the best man he could find for the job. He had indicated his estimation of

Bob earlier in the season when the pitcher was having his usual midsummer problems and a sportswriter asked if he contemplated taking Gibson out of the rotation for a while. Keane replied, "If we're gonna win at all it will be with Gibson."

That's how Keane felt now, in the ninth inning of the seventh game of the World Series.

He didn't falter in his faith even when Clete Boyer and Phil Linz homered to cut the Cardinals' margin to 7-5. The situation, with two out, was Bobby Richardson in the batter's box and Roger Maris on deck. Richardson had already set a new Series record with 13 hits; Maris was a home-run threat.

In this clutch situation Bob called upon all his reserve. He got Richardson on a pop fly to Dal Maxvill at second, and the Cardinals exploded in wild celebration. They were champions!

Gibson not only won two of the Cardinals' four victories, but he also set a new Series record with 31 strikeouts. Among his many rewards was a Corvette sports car, given by *Sport* magazine annually to the Series' Most Valuable Player.

Gibson just seemed to get better and better each year. He began the 1965 season by winning eight straight, then ran into difficulties and was 10-7 at the All-Star break.

He pitched in that All-Star Game, with the expected Gibson touch. The first five National League pitchers were Juan Marichal, Jim Maloney, Don Drysdale, Sandy Koufax and Dick Farrell. Gibson came on to pitch the last two innings and protect a 6-5 lead. He held the American League to two hits and struck out three, closing the game by fanning Harmon Killebrew and Joe Pepitone.

Joe Torre, the Braves' catcher who caught the entire

contest, said afterward that Gibson was the fastest pitcher in the game.

He came back to his early season form soon after the All-Star contest, won 9 of his last thirteen, and finished the season at 20–12 for his first 20-game season.

Again in 1966 a strong finish late in the season put him up among the game's leaders, with a 21–12 mark.

At the top of his form and at the top of the league, Bob came close to complete disaster in 1967. On July 15, owning a 10–6 record, his right leg was shattered by a line drive off the bat of Pittsburgh's Roberto Clemente.

And yet, in a fantastic exhibition of courage, Gibson remained in the game to pitch to three more batters before he collapsed!

Gloom settled over the Cardinals' clubhouse. They were leading the league—but now, without Gibson, their confidence was shaken.

Fortunately, the rest of the staff responded magnificently and plugged the gap. Nelson Briles came in out of the bullpen and became a starter, winning nine games in Bob's absence.

For fifty-two days Gibson was out of action. There was, of course, considerable speculation about his ability to come back after missing nearly eight weeks. It was recalled that after breaking his leg at the end of the 1962 season, he had started badly in 1963, favoring the recently healed member. What would he do now, without a winter of rest?

Gibson gave the answer on September 7, at Shea Stadium in New York. In his first start since the accident he beat the Mets, 9–2. Then he beat the Phillies twice, 6–0 and 5–1. The Braves beat him in his final start of the season, 2–1.

The Cardinals romped home to a pennant. It was apparent that Gibson was as good as new and ready for the World Series against the Red Sox.

Boston not only had the best-hitting team in the American League, led by Triple-Crown winner Carl Yastrzemski, it had a short left field wall that Red Sox batters regarded as being particularly friendly.

Gibson wasn't worried about it. No right-hand hitter in baseball could pull his fast one over the fence. He threw what was called a "heavy ball." Johnny Keane described it by saying, "It knocks the bat right out of a guy's hands." And slugger Tommy Davis once called Gibson's fast one a "radio ball." "You hear it but you don't see it," said Davis.

Bob beat the Red Sox in the first game, 2–1, spinning a six-hitter. Then he shut them out with a five-hitter in the fourth game, winning, 6–0. The Red Sox looked like a beaten crew then, the Cardinals leading 3–1 in the Series and looking for the clincher. But Boston fought back and won the next two, showing their hitting strength, sending three home runs over the left field wall in one inning in the sixth game for a new Series record.

The wall still didn't faze Bob. He was called upon, as he had been in 1964, to win the deciding contest. Facing him in the seventh game was Red Sox ace Jim Lonborg.

Before the game began, Boston's slugging first baseman, George Scott, boasted, "Gibson won't last five innings."

Scott was in error. Gibson lasted nine, hit a home run himself, and won his third game of the 1967 Series, his fifth straight complete Series game to tie Red Ruffing's old record. With poetic justice, he struck out Scott for his tenth strikeout and final out of the game.

Again the Most Valuable Player of the Series, Gibson won his second Corvette sports car from *Sport* magazine.

The way the 1968 season started for Gibson and the Cardinals, few baseball observers would have predicted the finish accurately. The Cardinals weren't hitting, and they weren't hitting especially behind Gibson.

The game on May 23 against the Dodgers was a typical example. Through eight innings Gibson had given up just one hit. But the hit drove in a run, and in the eighth Gibson left for a pinch hitter, trailing 1–0. His reliever allowed another run. He lost, 2–0.

Now, after nine starts, he owned the best earned-run average in the National League, a 1.33 mark. But his won-lost record was 3–4. In his four losses his teammates had given him just three runs—had given him just eleven altogether in his nine starts! Moreover, of the 17 runs he had allowed, only 12 were earned.

He lost his next game, too. Then on June 2 he beat the Mets, 6–3, and began an incredible winning streak of 15 games that didn't end until the Pirates beat him on August 24, 6–4. Even then he was stopped with the aid of three unearned runs.

In the course of the dramatic win streak he threw five straight shutouts. A wild pitch killed his chance to overtake Don Drysdale's record scoreless string, set just a few weeks earlier. By coincidence, it was Drysdale he beat, 5–1, that day. The run scored in the first inning. After Gibson got the first two Dodger hitters, Len Gabrielson and Tom Haller singled. Pitching to Ron Fairly, Bob threw a fast ball low and inside that hit the dirt, bounced off catcher Johnny Edwards' shinguards and kicked away, allowing Gabrielson to score from third.

In the Cardinals' clubhouse afterward, Gibson was lighthearted about the snap of his scoreless streak. When a sportswriter asked him if he thought the pressure of the streak had gotten to him, he scoffed. "Pressure?" Gibson replied. "Call it aggravation. There was more pressure on me when I was growing up as a kid." He was referring, of course, to his ghetto beginnings in Omaha.

When his winning streak was finally stopped in late August, he struck out 15 men in the game, giving him 129 strikeouts in his last 144 innings. In the course of the 15-game streak he allowed just 7 runs. He pitched 10 shutouts. Truly this was one of the great pitching performances in baseball history.

He wasn't finished with historic performances yet, however. The loss to Pittsburgh gave him an 18–6 record, and an incredible 1.07 ERA. Then he pitched two straight shutouts, giving him 20 victories and 12 shutouts.

In the closing moments of the Cardinals' dash to a second straight pennant, he won two more while losing three, for a 22–9 record. With a few breaks, fewer errors behind him and a bit more hitting, he could easily have been 31–0.

His effectiveness was record-breaking. Pitching 304⅔ innings, he gave up 38 earned runs for a new major league ERA record of 1.12. With 268 strikeouts he tied the National League record of six seasons with 200 or more strikeouts, held by Koufax and Drysdale.

Now there was the World Series, heralded as the Battle of the Pitchers: Gibson against Denny McLain, the Tigers' 31-game winner.

The first game was all Gibson's. It was said later that he might have set a new record for most standing ovations received in a single game, so responsive was the crowd to his performance. He shut out Detroit, 4–0.

With 14 strikeouts to his credit going into the ninth inning, Bob was one away from the Series record set by Koufax. Mickey Stanley opened the Tigers' ninth with a single. Then Gibson struck out Al Kaline on a one-and-two pitch to tie Sandy. Then he struck out Norm Cash to break the record. Finally he struck out Willie Horton to establish the new mark at 17 strikeouts.

The next duel between the two great pitchers again went to Gibson. This time McLain was severely cuffed. While Gibson gave up only five hits, struck out ten and allowed one run, the Cardinals jumped on McLain and a succession of relief hurlers for a 10–1 rout.

In the course of the victory, two more World Series records fell to Gibson. He hit a home run, becoming the only pitcher ever to hit two in World Series play. The victory was his seventh straight in Series competition, a new record.

The Cardinals now led, three games to one. When they greeted Mickey Lolich with a three-run outburst in the first inning of the fifth game, it looked like the championship for St. Louis. But Detroit came back to win, 5–3, and won again the next day, 13–1.

The Series was down to the seventh game. Again the call came for Gibson to win the big one. Mickey Lolich, also winner of two contests, got the call for Detroit.

For six innings the two aces dueled scorelessly. The Tigers had just one hit off Gibson. Then, with two down in the seventh, Norm Cash got the second hit, a single to right. Horton followed with a single through the infield to left, Cash stopping at second.

Jim Northrup hit a drive to center field. In went Curt Flood, then he stopped, slipped, and headed back to the wall. It was too late. The ball sailed over his head. Two runs scored. Northrup wound up on third. Bill Freehan doubled for the third run before Gibson retired the side.

The way Lolich was pitching, the Tigers didn't need any more than that. They scored one more in the ninth, and the Cardinals finally broke through with one in their half. But the victory and the championship belonged to Lolich and the Tigers.

In the clubhouse afterward, Bob took a philosophical view of his defeat. He didn't blame Flood for the play which opened the gates for the Tigers.

On the contrary, when Flood in fact took the blame himself, Gibson said the outfielder was being foolish. "Curt's a real pro," Bob said. "Curt would say it's his fault, because that's the kind of guy he is."

Then he added: "I thought I pitched well enough to win most games, but the other guy pitched a better game."

The Tigers took away his victory, but they couldn't take away the fact that even in defeat Gibson was breaking records. This one was his own. By striking out eight men in the seventh game he brought his Series total to a new record of 35—surpassing his 1964 mark of 31.

So ended a most remarkable year for Bob Gibson. It was an overall performance that won him the National League Most Valuable Player Award—and brought him a giant step closer to that eventual niche in the Hall of Fame.

Denny McLain ....

Denny McLain ●●●●●●●●●●●●●●●●●●●●●●●●●●●●●

He stands on the mound in a lopsided crouch, cap pulled low over his eyes, which peer out through contact lenses at the sign from his catcher. Then he winds up, kicks high. The left leg comes around, toe pointed at the plate like a ballet dancer. When he lets go of the ball the odds are heavily in favor of its crossing the plate in the strike zone, and equally heavy that the fast ball or hard slider will either be missed completely or be struck with little damaging effect.

The style of Denny McLain's pitching is classic, a delight to behold—unless you're one of his opponents.

Even such a nagging perfectionist as Tiger pitching coach Johnny Sain is awed at the delivery. Sain, who once did a famous double act with Warren Spahn on the old Boston Braves, said of McLain, "Denny's pitching is like I thought a big leaguer should pitch when I was a boy. With his kind of motion, I don't know why he can't be a good pitcher forever."

Only twenty-four years old at the end of the 1968 season, Denny certainly had many years ahead of him to justify such an extravagant prophecy. However, no matter how successful those future seasons might prove, it would be difficult to imagine a greater one than his 1968 campaign. Few people would dare to predict that Denny would ever match his dazzling 1968 performance.

Indeed, few were those who knew Denny during his minor league days who would have predicted his making the major leagues at all. And there was a time, when he was very young, that Denny himself entertained thoughts

119

of becoming a professional organist instead of a baseball player. (Now, of course, he's both.)

When he was a boy at Ascension grade school in Markham, Illinois, Denny divided his free time between the organ and sandlot baseball. His father coached him at both. Mr. McLain was by profession an insurance adjuster, but he earned extra money giving electric organ lessons. He had also been a pretty fair semipro shortstop in his youth.

The picture of Denny at an organ doesn't quite fit with the general image of him as a youngster. He was quick, independent, and sharp-tongued. He got into street fights. He argued with the sisters at Ascension grade school because he didn't like the blue bow tie they forced him to wear.

Yet he sincerely liked playing the organ. For a time he actually thought he would make music his career. There is a distinct possibility he might have done just that if he hadn't proved to be such a hotshot pitcher on the Little League team at Markham.

He was tremendously strong and fast for a Little League pitcher. Nobody could hit him. Hardly anybody could catch him. His own brother, Tim, caught him for a while, but Denny boasted later that he threw so hard he knocked Tim over. Later, Tim became a pitcher in the White Sox farm system.

From Ascension grade school Denny went on to Mt. Carmel High, known as Chicago's "Little Notre Dame." He was not an interested student. He got by. He was as good as he needed to be to pass—an attitude he carried over later to his professional pitching.

It was at Carmel that Denny realized he had the actual potential to become a major league pitcher. Throwing nothing but fast balls—he didn't own a curve—he was the sensation of the high school league. He won 38 games and lost 7 as a high school pitcher. At the same time, he was playing around Chicago in several amateur leagues at once.

He could have had his pick of several college athletic scholarships when he left Mt. Carmel, but by now Denny's mind was fixed on baseball. As soon as he graduated he signed with the White Sox. They shipped him at once to Harlan, Kentucky, a Class D Appalachian League club.

Denny was an instant sensation—in more ways than one. He pitched his first game for Harlan on June 28, 1962, against Salem. The ink on his high school diploma was barely dry. Yet he came in and pitched a no-hitter.

You can't do better than that in your first professional baseball game.

Denny didn't stay around Harlan very long though. He loudly proclaimed that it was a "hick town" (Harlan's population was 4000) and complained about the facilities at his hotel.

He lost his second start, then was shipped off to Clinton, Iowa, in the Midwestern League. He wasn't overly impressed with Clinton, either. On the other hand, Ira Hutchinson, the Clinton manager, wasn't overly impressed with Denny. For one thing, the youngster was undisciplined. He broke regulations and club curfew. Furthermore, he was no big deal on the mound. He won four and lost seven for Clinton.

Thus, despite his no-hitter debut as a professional, he was just 5–8 in his first season—and he hadn't made many friends or well-wishers.

In the upper reaches of the White Sox management, there was a tendency to overlook Denny's transgressions. There were men there who believed his potential was worth tolerance. Accordingly, in spring training of 1963, they thought of bringing him up for a brief look that season, or certainly testing him in stiffer minor league company. However, there was another promising pitcher in camp that spring, Bruce Howard. Chicago's manager, Al Lopez, couldn't make up his mind which of the two he favored for the big jump. He let the two pitchers battle it out in an intrasquad game. Howard won, 2-1.

Such are the vagaries of baseball. Howard won the jump—and disappeared into the White Sox machinery forever. McLain lost. He was picked up on waivers by Detroit that April—and became one of the great stars of the game. One wonders what Al Lopez was thinking during the 1968 season.

McLain improved tremendously in 1963. He was leading the Northern League, playing with Duluth, working on a 13-2 season when the Tigers shipped him over to Knoxville, in the Sally League. He won five and lost four. Then, at the tail end of the season, the Tigers called him up for a taste of big league competition. "A cup of coffee," major league players call such an opportunity.

Denny still threw only fast balls. A few days before he was given his first start, Denny was taken aside by manager Charley Dressen and instructed in throwing the curve. On September 21, at Tiger Stadium, he was given the ball and sent in—against the White Sox.

The opportunity was too good for a strong-headed lad like Denny McLain to miss. He struck out eight batters, hit a home run, and beat the White Sox, 4-3.

He was 2-1 with the parent club that September. Back trouble and a tendency to throw too many home-run balls kept him in the dugout most of 1964. Dividing his time between Syracuse and Detroit he had a 7-6 season.

Nevertheless manager Dressen decided to give him a

full crack at making the team in 1965. Denny started off badly, won only one of his four starts—a 4–0 shutout of Washington. Then things began to fall into place. Called upon in relief in June, he suddenly felt a rhythm come into his pitching. He had found, as pitchers call it, his "groove."

Dave Wickersham was the starting pitcher against Boston that night. But with three runs across and only one out, Denny was called in to take over. He struck out the first two hitters, to end the rally. In the second inning he struck out the side. In the third inning he struck out the first two men for a string of seven consecutive strikeouts —a new major league record for relief pitching, and tying the American League consecutive strikeout record by any pitcher set by Ryne Duren in 1961.

Denny went on to strike out fourteen men in six and two-thirds innings before giving way to a pinch hitter in the seventh. Ironically the Tigers rallied in the eighth inning to win, but Denny, of course, did not get credit for the victory.

He did, however, win eight straight games after that before the Yankees beat him late in July. He became the ace of the Tigers' staff, finishing the season as No. 2 percentage winner in the American League, winning 16 and losing 6 for a .727 average. His 2.62 earned run average put him seventh on the list.

One of the brightest young stars in baseball, Denny, twenty-two years old, was picked to be the opening pitcher for the American League All-Stars in the summer of 1966. His performance was perfect. He retired nine men in a row and struck out Willie Mays, Joe Torre and Hank Aaron, three of the toughest hitters in baseball. From there he continued on to a 20–14 season, becoming one of the youngest pitchers ever to hit 20 victories in a season.

Comparing this accomplishment with the great pitchers of recent years, Denny at twenty-two did it five years sooner than Sandy Koufax, four years sooner than Don Drysdale and Warren Spahn, seven years sooner than Bob Gibson and ten years sooner than Whitey Ford.

Denny slid backward in 1967. Some said his problem was the same one that had bothered him in the latter part of 1966—overreliance on his change-up pitch. It was true that this pitch was being hit out of the park more than any other, and was making Denny the most generous homer-ball pitcher in baseball. But there were other factors as well. He appeared to be distracted by personal and business problems. He wasn't concentrating on baseball. He feuded with the Detroit fans and the press. He even claimed to be bothered with his vision; he wore thick-rimmed glasses on the field.

Then a shoulder injury bothered his motion. And finally, late in September, he dislocated two toes on his left foot in an accident at home. He was finished for the season with a 17–16 record.

Whatever bothered Denny in 1967 he managed to dispose of in time for the next season. The personal problems he dealt with over the winter months. Then he came to spring training like a true Tiger and went to work. He traded his eyeglasses for contact lenses, and claimed he could focus better on the target. He worked with coach Sain on a new, hard slider, convinced at last that the change-up he liked so much was a major cause of his proclivity for the home-run pitch.

Now putting together all the elements he owned, Denny began the performance of a lifetime.

After two no-decision contests to open the season,

Denny McLain

he won five straight before the Orioles beat him. He was 14–2 by the end of June. This was an incredible pace, and, with 20 wins a foregone conclusion, the press and the fans began asking the obvious question: Could Denny win 30 games? Nobody had won 30 games in the major leagues since Dizzy Dean's big season of 1934.

True, the Tigers were hitting behind Denny, as they drove with determination toward the pennant. But Denny didn't need all of it. The home run pitch had disappeared with the change-up, which he now threw rarely. Gone, too, were most of the bases on balls.

When he beat the Orioles, 9–0, on July 27 for one of the earliest 20-win attainments in baseball history, he had lost only 3 games, struck out 173 in 210 innings and walked only 36! His earned run average was 2.10.

His win total went to 25 before he was beaten again. The White Sox clobbered him, then he lost a 2–1 decision to the Yankees. Righting himself, he beat the Angels, 6–1, and then made the dash for the magic number. On September 10 he beat the Angels again for his 29th win against 5 defeats.

Four days later, on September 14, the stage was set. The pennant race by then was conceded to the Tigers. All eyes were on McLain.

Could the brash young hurler, a mere twenty-four years old, with just three full seasons of major league ball behind him, accomplish what no pitcher had since 1934—and indeed none but a few of the masters had *ever* accomplished?

Such was the interest all over America that the game between the Oakland A's and the Tigers was televised nationally. Dizzy Dean, who had done it last in 1934, was on hand to watch.

The pregame activities were the same as they would have been on any other afternoon, with several notable exceptions. There were a few more reporters in the clubhouse before the game, asking Denny how he felt. "I feel fine," he said. "I guess I'll get a little nervous when I get out there. But I don't feel anything yet."

Later, when he went out onto the field, and the early arrivals in Tiger Stadium recognized him, a round of cheers rang out. Denny smiled. He had experienced his share of jeers, too, especially after he had publicly criticized some of the Tiger fans for being disloyal.

As he stood by the batting cage, waiting to hit, he noticed Oakland catcher Jim Pagliaroni parading around with a sign, reading: "Chuck Dobson goes for No. 12 today." Denny smiled again. No use pretending this day wasn't something special. Or at least he could so hope.

For three innings Dobson and Denny matched scoreless frames. But Reggie Jackson of the A's homered with a man on to give Oakland a 2–0 lead in the fourth. The Tigers came back in their half with a three-run homer by Norm Cash, and Denny had a lead.

It was not one of his better days. He lost his lead the next inning on a walk, a sacrifice and a single, and with two out in the sixth, Jackson hit his second homer for a 4–3 Oakland lead.

Denny held then. For Oakland, Diego Segui was now in the game to hold off the Tigers.

Al Kaline opened the Tigers' ninth by drawing a walk. The fans in the grandstand began howling for a rally. On the bench, Denny sat quietly, watching and waiting. Dick McAuliffe fouled off two sacrifice bunt attempts, then popped out foul, but Mickey Stanley came through with a single through the box, Kaline racing to third.

With the infield drawn in for a play at the plate, Jim

Northrup bounced to first base. Danny Cater had plenty of time for the play at home, but he threw wildly. Kaline scored the tying run and Stanley wound up on third.

Now it was up to Willie Horton. Only the runner on third counted—Stanley. The outfield played Willie shallow, the infield was pulled in. A long fly ball would do just as well as a hit.

The count went to two-and-two on Horton. The tension in Tiger Stadium was terrific.

On the two-two pitch Horton swung. The drive was a long one to left. Jim Gosger went back for it—but the ball sailed over his outstretched glove.

Denny McLain had his thirtieth win!

The rest of the season, even the World Series that followed, exciting as it was, seemed little more than the necessary technicalities to finish the season after that dramatic afternoon.

Denny split his last two decisions, beating the Yankees, 6–2, then losing to Baltimore, 2–1.

In the victory over the Yankees, Denny generously helped Mickey Mantle to a step upward in the record books. He was coasting along on a four-hitter, winning 6–1, when Mantle came to bat in the eighth inning. It was Mickey's final appearance of the year at Tiger Stadium; for all anyone knew, his last appearance for all time.

A standing ovation greeted Mantle as he came up to hit. Denny waited until the cheers subsided, then he threw two inside fast balls past Mantle for two strikes. Mickey jokingly motioned for Denny to throw the ball farther out over the plate. To his surprise, McLain actually did groove a pitch for him. Mantle swung and belted the ball on a line into the bleachers.

As he trotted around the bases to another standing

ovation, Mantle yelled, "Thanks!" to Denny. It was the Yankee slugger's 17th homer of the season, and his 535th lifetime homer, breaking his tie with Jimmy Fox for third place on the all-time list.

The World Series, featuring the much-awaited clash between McLain and the Cardinals' ace Bob Gibson, was won by the Tigers. But the private duel was won by Gibson. Denny lost to him twice.

The Series wasn't a complete bust for Denny, however. With the Cardinals leading, three games to two, and the championship in their grasp, Denny came back to stop them cold, and the Tigers rose up in wrath behind him. While his teammates racked up a record 10-run inning in the third, Denny scattered nine hits, striking out seven for a 13–1 victory.

The next day Mickey Lolich beat Gibson, 4–1. The Tigers were World's Champions of 1968.

And Denny McLain was the champion pitcher of the year.

He won it all. Thirty-one games, and then after the World Series he became the first pitcher ever to be voted, *unanimously,* both the Cy Young Award and the Most Valuable Player Award.

In a way, a season like the 1968 one could be a mixed blessing for a twenty-four-year-old pitcher. To an older hurler, perhaps at the peak of a long career, such a season could be considered a fitting climax.

But where does Denny McLain go from 1968? He knows that everything he accomplishes in the future will be measured against that fantastic season. It can prove a rewarding challenge, or an anchor dragging behind him, a crippling burden. Roger Maris experienced some of the latter problem after he broke Babe Ruth's homer record in 1961 with his 61 homers. He was expected to measure up to that miraculous feat thereafter—an unfair target set up by unthinking people. When, of course, he couldn't repeat, he was practically tormented right out of New York.

Denny McLain may face a similar situation. However he reacts to it, he will always know that for one season, at least, he put together everything and reached a mark unseen in baseball for almost forty years.

And after all, as his coach Johnny Sain said, with his style, there was no reason why Denny McLain couldn't be a good pitcher forever.

And Long, Long Ago ....

Wide World photos

Grover Cleveland Alexander

Grover Cleveland Alexander

When you're a teen-age boy in a family of twelve children, trying to scratch out a living on a Nebraska farm, you work hard. From dawn to dusk you plow, pitchfork, see to the livestock and anything else that has to be done. And, if you're a teen-ager in the year 1905 in America, plowing means walking behind mules—not riding a tractor.

You get strong, working like that. You get leg muscles that never quit and arms that never tire. You also get an itch to make an extra dollar somewhere—anywhere, where the work might be just a little more fun than following a mule across a patch of Nebraska corn field.

That's how Grover Cleveland Alexander—"Ol' Pete" and "Alex the Great" they called him later—got started in baseball.

Alex started as an outfielder around St. Paul, near where he farmed. Because he was strong and could run and hit, he was much in demand by local semiprofessional teams that played on weekends, often to pass-the-hat admissions and winning club take all. If he picked up an extra dollar or two that way on a weekend, that was fine with Alex. The family sorely needed a bit of hard cash, and anyway, baseball was fun, not work.

For two or three years, from the time he was sixteen, Alex picked up extra money this way, playing for small, independent teams, the local firehouse, the ice company, for anybody, earning nickels and dimes as an outfielder.

Baseball legend has it that lightning struck Alex one

day while he was patrolling the deep grass for a team in Elba, Nebraska—the lightning that dramatically changes a man's entire life pattern. Elba was being murdered that afternoon. The score was 15–1 against them, and it was only the fifth inning. The Elba manager, fresh out of pitchers to throw into the cauldron, waved in his outfielder.

"You've got the strongest arm on the team, kid," he said to the youngster. "Just try to get the ball over the plate."

Alex took the ball from his manager and went to the mound. He stood there, uncertain, a tall, freckle-faced, typical farm lad in cut-down denim overalls for a uniform. Then, with a shrug, he began to throw.

And how he threw! The lad didn't know a curve when he saw one. All he could do was throw the ball in there, hard and true. But not a man got a hit off him for the rest of the game!

According to the legend, Alex got a five-dollar bonus for that performance. In any case, he was a pitcher from that day onward.

Before long word got around Nebraska that there was a real pitcher at Elba. And in 1908, when he was twenty-one, he was offered fifty dollars a month to pitch for a team in Central City. This was real money to Alex and his family. It also meant he was a professional baseball player. Central City was not in organized baseball, as such, but it was a professional team, and many of its players were quickly snapped up by teams in organized ball.

Alex was grabbed almost as soon as he started pitching for Central City. Before the season was over he was signed for 1909 with the Galesburg team of the Illinois-Missouri League. No formal farm affiliations were in practice then; he was not, that is, signed by a major league franchise and started in Galesburg, as would have been done in modern baseball. In those early days of the game, the lower leagues signed players themselves, traded and sold amongst themselves and to the major league teams.

Alex was ecstatic with his good fortune. Galesburg gave him a hundred dollars a month, which practically made him the breadwinner of his entire family. He took care of his parents and his brothers and sister, too, generously sharing his earnings with them.

As good luck struck him in Galesburg, so did misfortune—almost cutting short his career before it had really begun. Hit in the head with a thrown ball late in the season, he was unconscious for almost three days. Afterward, he suffered from headaches, dizziness and double vision. He could pitch no more that season, but already he had established himself with a 15–8 mark, and with 198 strikeouts in 219 innings pitched.

While sitting out the rest of the 1909 season on the bench, he suddenly found that he had been sold to Indianapolis. There, manager Joe Carr, unaware that Alex was still suffering from the injury's aftereffects, let him pitch. Alex felt an obligation to try. When he hit the first batter he faced, he took himself out of the game and explained fully to his manager.

"I thought you knew when you bought my contract," he said to Carr.

"Nobody told me a durned thing," Carr said. Without bitterness, however, Carr sent the young pitcher home to rest out the remainder of the season. Then he, too, anxious to unload what appeared to be a liability, sold Alex to Syracuse, in the New York State League.

Carr should have had more patience. In Syracuse, Alex's vision cleared. Completely free from complaints, he turned in a fantastic season at Syracuse, winning 29 games and losing 14.

He was ready for the big time, and the Philadelphia Phillies bought out his contract. Now, as a major league pitcher, he was given $250 a month.

The Phillies were not a hitting team, yet Alex, a raw rookie, still learning to throw the curve, turned in one of the most remarkable freshman seasons in the annals of baseball. He won 28, lost only 13, and struck out 227 men!

One of Alex's victories that season was of historical note. Late in the campaign he was matched against Denton (Cy) Young, forty-four years old, with the all-time major league record of 511 victories. Then with the Boston Nationals, Young had a 4–4 record in this, his fade-out year. This was, too, his last game. He wanted a win to make his last appearance a winning one, and his last season a winning one.

Facing the youthful Alex, the aged veteran put on an amazing performance. But Alex stayed right with him. For eleven innings each man hurled shutout ball. Finally, in the twelfth, the Phillies broke through for a run, giving Alex a 1–0 victory.

In a way, Alex was sorry to win. He knew how much that victory would have meant to the great Cy Young. But he knew, too, that to have pitched at anything less than his maximum efficiency to help Young would have been wrong. Certainly, had he done so, and Young suspected it, the victory would have been a meaningless one.

As it turned out, Young came back to the clubhouse after the game and congratulated his rookie opponent. He said to manager Charley Dooin, "Red, this boy is going to be one of the best. You wait and see."

Alex had fine season after fine season, but he didn't

really blossom fully until 1915. Twenty-eight years old by then, he was in the prime of physical life. He won 31 games for the Phillies that year, following that with 33 victories in 1916 and 30 in 1917.

He set a few major league records in those three exciting years.

In 1915 he won 4 one-hit games; in 1916 he pitched 16 shutouts; in 1916 and again in 1917 he won two games in one day. In addition, in 1915 he set a National League earned-run average record with 1.22.

Still at the height of his career, he was traded to the Cubs after the 1917 season. There he fell afoul of the strict disciplinarian methods of manager Joe McCarthy, who later was to win greater glory as a manager of the Yankees. But now McCarthy was piloting a somewhat less successful Chicago team. He was never a liberal manager in any case, but a stern, humorless, yet fair taskmaster. Alex, on the other hand, had just a bit of rogue in him. He didn't care for training rules, he was an umpire baiter, in a good-humored way, and he had a habit of double-crossing his catchers, just for fun.

After eight years of this, McCarthy's thin patience wore through, and the men had a row. It was no secret now in the league that McCarthy was looking to get rid of Alex. Most of the league's managers, however, mistook Alex's 15-11 record in 1925 and McCarthy's impatience as a sign that Ol' Pete was through.

One man didn't think so. That was Bill Killefer, a coach with the Cardinals. Killefer, once Alex's catcher on the Phillies and traded with him to the Cubs, believed he still had good years left. It was his opinion that McCarthy did not have the temperament to get the best out of a man like Alex.

Killefer advised manager Rogers Hornsby of his feelings. Hornsby was skeptical. Still, the Cardinals were pennant contenders, and Hornsby could well do with a little pitching help. And perhaps, too, he remembered back some ten years before, to 1915, when he was rookie shortstop with the Cardinals and Alex was a big winner with the Phillies.

Hornsby was still a questionable item then, in fact, was in danger of being shipped down to the minor leagues. One day, hitting against Alexander, he was struck out twice in succession. His spirits were flagging.

At that moment this same Killefer and Alexander got together—or so Hornsby heard it later—and decided that with the game already in the bag they would let the kid hit one next time around, to boost his spirits.

Alex grooved a fast ball for him, and sure enough Hornsby rapped the pitch for a double, breaking him out of a prolonged slump.

And so Hornsby agreed to take Alex onto the Cardinals. It was a gamble, but Hornsby was a gambler.

Alex responded to the new atmosphere and his realliance with Killefer. The first game he pitched was sweet revenge—he beat the Cubs. He went on to win eight more for the Cardinals, helping them tremendously as they scrambled to the pennant. Alex finished that season with a 12–10 record.

Now came the World Series. Facing the Cardinals were Babe Ruth and Company—the great Yankees of 1926. Murderer's Row, the middle of their lineup was called, with Ruth, Bob Meusel and Lou Gehrig batting 3–4–5. Not many American League pitchers got through those three unscathed.

The Yankees won the first game, beating Willie Sherdel. Then Hornsby called on thirty-nine-year-old Alex to even the score.

"Don't worry about me, Rog, I won't let you down," Alex said.

Alex stifled the big Yankee hitters the next day on four hits, winning, 6–2, retiring the last 21 men in order. The Yankees took the next two out of three, led in the Series three games to two, and needed just the clincher. Again Hornsby called on Alex, and again he beat the Yankees, 10–2.

The Series was even now. In the clubhouse after the Cardinals' clutch victory, manager Hornsby took Alex aside for a chat. "Alex," he said, "if you want to celebrate tonight I wouldn't blame you. But go easy. I may need you tomorrow."

Alex agreed.

Jesse Haines started the seventh game for the Cardinals. Waite Hoyt was on the mound for the Yankees. Early in the game Hornsby sent Alex down to the bullpen, but with orders to help Willie Sherdel and Herman Bell warm up. "You keep an eye on 'em and if I need help you tell me which one looks best," Hornsby said.

The game developed into a tough battle. Ruth got the Yankees out in front with a home run in the third inning, his fourth homer of the Series. The Cardinals rallied in the fourth, scoring three times, but the Yankees got one run back in the sixth.

Haines, a knuckleball thrower, now came up with a blister on the index finger of his pitching hand. He walked Earle Combs to open the seventh inning. Mark Koenig sacrificed. Hornsby ordered an intentional pass to Ruth. Meusel hit into a force play for the second out. Again taking no chances, Hornsby ordered Gehrig passed, loading the bases.

At that crucial point, aware of Haines' blistering finger, the Cardinals' manager called for Ol' Pete.

Alex, who had been warming up Sherdel and Bell, had no idea Hornsby might want him in relief. He had, after all, gone nine tough innings the day before. He wasn't properly warmed up, therefore. Still, he didn't say anything, just took the ball from Haines and prepared to pitch to Tony Lazzeri with the bases loaded.

A dangerous batter in the clutch, Lazzeri swung at Alex's curve and missed. Then he caught a fast ball and lined it foul down the left field line.

Alex shook his head. "No more fast balls for you," he said to himself. With that he came back with another curve. Lazzeri swung and missed for strike three!

Alex was out of that jam. But there were two more innings to go. Calmly, without even a day's rest, the thirty-nine-year-old pitching marvel breezed through the Yankee hitters. They went down one-two-three in the eighth. With two out in the ninth, he walked Ruth, but the Babe was cut down trying to steal.

The game was over. The Cardinals had won their first World's Championship.

That 1926 World Series was the climactic high point of Alex's grand career. He came back with another fine season in 1927, at forty, when most players long have hung up their spikes. He won 21 and lost 10.

That was his last big year. Even his stalwart arm couldn't hold out indefinitely. He pitched two more years for the Cardinals, went back to the Phillies for a year, then lingered on with Dallas in the Texas League, where he won one and lost two, a forty-three-year-old shadow of his former greatness.

It was a pity, a shame, that Alex could not spend the rest of his years somewhere in organized baseball, or at least in respectful retirement. But he had poor luck, and suffered from ill health.

Grover Cleveland Alexander, Ol' Pete, Alex the Great, was elected to the Hall of Fame in 1938. Among his many career highlights is his lifetime total of 373 victories, tying him with Christy Mathewson for the National League record.

In 1950, back home in St. Paul, Nebraska, he died of a heart attack at sixty-three.

Wide World photos

Walter Johnson ....

Walter Johnson ••••••••••••••••••••••••••••

Walter Johnson, "The Big Train," was considered by many to have been the fastest pitcher in the history of baseball. Many are the legends about his speed, about the great control he had over his sweeping fast ball, which he threw with a smooth, half-sidearm motion.

It was said that batters swung at his pitches as he let the ball go, knowing they wouldn't see the ball as it crossed the plate, knowing it would be a fast ball (Johnson didn't bother with a curve at all) and hoping by chance they'd hit it.

Umpires, too, had problems seeing Johnson's bullets. According to one story, Johnson had two outs and two strikes on an Athletics batter in the ninth inning when he put just a little extra speed on his fast ball. The pitch socked into the catcher's mitt with a loud smack. Johnson began walking off the mound. "Strike three!" the umpire called.

The batter turned around. "I couldn't see that ball and you couldn't see that ball," he said to the umpire. "How do you know it was a strike?"

The umpire shrugged and indicated Johnson's retreating figure with a nod of his head. "Maybe so," he said. "But if Walter thinks it was a strike, then it was a strike! You're out!"

Al Schacht, a pitching teammate of Johnson's, but better known later as a comedian, "The Clown Prince of Baseball," used to tell another Johnson story. According to Schacht, umpire Billy Evans once called a game "on account of darkness" when the sun was still shining brightly because Johnson's fast balls repeatedly got through a rookie catcher and were bouncing off his shins. The record book tells Johnson's story equally well, though with less humor. For twenty-one years The Big Train toiled for the Washington Senators, who were second-division dwellers for fifteen of those years. Only twice did they win the pennant. Yet Johnson compiled a lifetime record of 416 victories, second only to Cy Young's 511-win record. He participated in 60 1–0 games, winning 40 and losing 20. He holds the major league record for most shutouts in a season, 16, most lifetime shutouts, 113, and is second only to Drysdale in consecutive shutout innings, 56.

Born in Kansas in 1887, Johnson didn't begin to play baseball until his family moved to California. There, in Fullerton, he discovered the game, and played for his high school team. He wanted to turn professional upon graduation, but couldn't land a spot with any of the Pacific Coast teams.

Finally he took a job as a miner in Weiser, Idaho, largely because the mines had a well-known semipro team. Actually, it was more likely the other way around: Weiser had a good semipro baseball team whose players also worked the iron mines.

In either case, Johnson did well with Weiser, winning the first three games he pitched, and going on to a winning season. He knew he had made a hit with the local fans that year when they began calling him "pardner" instead of "sonny." The following season, he was 13–2 when scout Cliff Blankenship of the Washington Senators was sent out to Idaho to sign him.

Johnson was taking no chances. He refused to sign a contract unless it included a return ticket to California —just in case he didn't make it in the big leagues. There was no hint of eccentricity in Johnson's demand. He was a genuinely modest young man, and while confident he had the makings of a big leaguer, he wasn't sure that a couple of seasons of semipro ball were experience enough.

Blankenship agreed to his terms, and, according to legend, they signed an agreement on a piece of brown wrapping paper from the local butcher shop.

He made his debut in Washington on August 2, 1907, against the Detroit Tigers. The Senators couldn't have found him a tougher team to face for a curtain raiser. The Tigers had heard about the fast-balling young right-hander from Idaho, and they were ready for him.

Johnson didn't disappoint the fans who came out to see his smoking fast ball. He had it, and he began to throw it right past the big Tiger hitters. But Detroit's hitters were more than just sluggers; they were smart. When they found they couldn't belt Johnson's fast one, two of them, Ty Cobb and Wahoo Sam Crawford, began to bunt. Johnson's inexperience cost him dearly. He fell all over himself trying to field the ball, and the gleeful Tigers bunted him crazy. They beat him, too, 3–2.

For a nineteen-year-old semipro from Idaho, however, it was not a defeat to complain about.

Washington was a dismal team when Johnson came to them, perennial cellar dwellers or just a step above. He started off slowly with them, gained stride gradually, and in 1910 and 1911 won 25 games, though the club finished seventh both times (this was in the eight-team league days).

When he got a little hitting behind him, Johnson was virtually unbeatable. As testimony, when Washington rose from the depths in 1912 and 1913 to finish in second place, Johnson came up with seasons of 32–12 and then the best of his career, 36–7. In that latter season, too, he fashioned 12 shutouts, and set a major league earned-run mark of 1.14!

Johnson was not only one of the most respected but also the most loved pitcher in baseball—and this in an era when ballplayers were a much rougher breed than they are today. Johnson was unique for those days, in that he had no temperament, held no grudges, and never complained about anything—including errors that lost him ball games.

Once he was locked in an eleven-inning duel with Boston, when outfielder Zeb Milan (a former teammate at Weiser) let a ball roll through his legs for a score that lost the game. In the clubhouse afterward a teammate patted his shoulder, remarking that it was a tough way to lose.

"Well," Johnson said, "Zeb doesn't do that very often, you know."

Another time he was forced to strike out four men in one inning, when, after whipping a third strike past the third man, the catcher let the ball get away and the batter reached first. Afterward, Johnson remarked, grinning, "Well, at least that gets me into the record books, don't it?"

He had the habit, too, of easing up on young hitters when the outcome of the game was no longer a question. Similarly, he would give the poorer hitters a chance, too, when he knew the game was as good as won. Some might say this is not evidence of a sincere competitor, but it was not so in Johnson's case. When a game was close, or he faced a good hitter under any circumstances, he was the toughest competitor in baseball. It was just that, with his pleasant nature, he disliked embarrassing anybody, even if it was an enemy batter.

According to Zeb Milan, who was his roommate

through fifteen years of semipro and professional baseball, Johnson "had the finest disposition of any ballplayer who ever lived."

The Senators didn't win a pennant until 1924. Johnson, thirty-seven years old by then, still managed to lead the league's pitchers that season with 23 wins against 7 losses, 6 shutouts, 158 strikeouts and a 2.72 ERA.

It was unfortunate for Big Train that he got his World Series chance so late in his career. The Giants beat him in his first start, 4–3, though it took them twelve innings to do it. But it was apparent that the once blinding speed was not all there. In the fifth game, with the Series at two-all, Johnson tried again, and again he was beaten. Washington won the sixth game, 2–1, and the Series went to the final game.

On the train ride from New York to Washington the night before the final contest, a dejected Walter Johnson sat by himself, tears in his eyes, a frustrated and hurt man. He was angry at himself, too, for failing, after so many years of waiting, to win a World Series game. He felt he had let his teammates down miserably.

As he sat there, Clark Griffith, the team's owner, came to him and said, "Don't think about it anymore, Walter. You're a great pitcher. We all know it."

Johnson nodded his thanks, and Griffith went on. "Go home and get to bed early," he said. "We may need you tomorrow."

The Washington ball park was jammed to overflowing the next day—the last game of the team's first World Series. Even Calvin Coolidge, the President of the United States, was on hand.

Manager Bucky Harris started Curley Ogden, against Virgil Barnes for the Giants. Ogden was followed by George Mogridge and then Firpo Marberry as the

Giants took a 3–1 lead. In the bottom of the eighth Washington tied the score. Marberry was gone for a pinch hitter. Harris needed another relief man. He turned to Johnson, who was sitting on the bench.

"Walter," he said. "You're the best we got. We win or lose with you."

The huge crowd was electrified when Johnson went out to the mound. This was a moment of high drama. The aging veteran, in the twilight of a grand career, twice beaten in the Series, was being called upon to save the day for his team.

He didn't have it easy. He got Freddie Lindstrom to open the ninth, but then Frankie Frisch tripled. Ross Young was intentionally passed to set up a double play. Bearing down with all he had, Johnson struck out George Kelly and retired "Irish" Meusel on a ground ball to third.

In the tenth he walked Hack Wilson. Then he struck out Travis Jackson, and Hank Gowdy lined back to the box to start a double play.

The eleventh inning was the toughest of all. Heinie Groh opened the inning with a pinch-hit double. Lindstrom sacrificed him to third. Now Johnson was in deep trouble indeed. Up came Frankie Frisch. Johnson struck him out. Then he walked Ross Young intentionally. And he struck out Kelly again.

In the twelfth inning—trouble again. Meusel led off with a single. But again the stout-hearted Johnson reached back for a bit of extra strength. He struck out Hack Wilson, and retired Jackson and Gowdy easily to stifle the threat.

The Senators, meanwhile, were getting nowhere with a succession of Giant relief pitchers.

Their half of the twelfth began no differently. With

one out, Muddy Ruel lifted an easy foul behind the plate. But Gowdy stepped on his mask, lost his footing and dropped the ball. Reprieved, Ruel promptly doubled. Johnson, hitting for himself, grounded to Jackson at shortstop. Coming down off second in a feint toward third, Ruel partially blocked Jackson's vision. The shortstop fumbled, Ruel went back to second and Johnson was safe at first on the error.

Leadoff man Earl McNeely came up and hit a ground ball right at third baseman Fred Lindstrom. A groan went up from the crowd. It looked like an easy double-play ball. Lindstrom went down for the bouncer— when suddenly it hit a pebble, took a big hop over his head and rolled into left field!

Ruel, running all the way, made it around to score, giving Johnson the victory and Washington its first World's Championship.

For hours afterward the city's frenzied fans celebrated, dancing around the stadium, pouring out into the streets and parading on into the night.

Johnson and his wife went to a quiet restaurant for dinner, for their own, private celebration of his victory. But somehow his many friends and Washington fans discovered where he was. During the course of the meal more than 200 telegrams were delivered to his table.

He had one more big year after that, leading Washington to its second straight pennant, winning 20 games while losing 7. This time he won his first two World Series starts, beating the Pirates 4–1, then 4–0. However, this time it was his sad fate to lose the deciding game, 9–7. The finale was played through intermittent rain, and he couldn't keep the handle on his control.

Of his many great pitching performances, which include a 1–0 no-hitter against Boston in 1920, one of the most memorable is the game he pitched on opening day of the 1926 season.

Pitching the opening game was a tradition for Johnson. It had begun for him back in 1910, the first year it became tradition, too, for the President of the United States to throw out the first ball. William Howard Taft was President that first time, and Johnson threw a one-hit shutout against the Athletics in honor of the occasion.

It might have been a no-hitter, too. The only hit came on a fly ball by Home Run Baker. It was an easy chance, but Doc Gessler, the Washington right fielder, stumbled chasing the ball, and it dropped safely for a double.

Now it was 1926, and Big Train was opening his twentieth season of baseball for Washington. He was thirty-nine years old. His opponent, the great knuckleball artist Ed Rommel (later an umpire), was twenty-nine. Rommel also had behind him a strong hitting team with such men as Mickey Cochrane, Al Simmons, Joe Hauser and Max Bishop in the lineup.

Johnson and Rommel linked up in a tremendous pitching duel. The powerhouse Athletics' sluggers were held to stray singles by Johnson. The Senators weren't doing any better with Rommel's dancing knuckler.

At the end of nine innings the game was a scoreless tie. On the contest raged, through the tenth, the eleventh, the twelfth. The crowd cheered and groaned and yelled for the Senators to get Johnson a run. How long could his old arm hold out against the A's powerful array?

Through the thirteenth and fourteenth. And Johnson set the A's down again in the fifteenth, one-two-three.

Bucky Harris got a rally going in the bottom of the fifteenth with a single. The crowd cheered. Then they screamed madly as Goose Goslin doubled him to third. Joe Harris followed with another single and Bucky romped home with the Senators' winning run.

The 1–0, fifteen-inning victory was the last of the great Johnson performances, and therefore all the more memorable. Johnson himself, in later years, talked about the game as his masterpiece.

He completed the 1926 season with a 15–16 average, fading in 1927 to 5–6 before retiring from active play at the age of forty.

For many years afterward Johnson remained in baseball as a manager. First with Newark, of the International League, then Washington, and finally with Cleveland. He was not much of a success as a manager. His mild manner and forgiving nature were not compatible with the duties and responsibilities of the leader of a baseball team.

He was elected to the Hall of Fame in 1936. After a brief career in politics following that, Johnson became ill. The once strong body wasted away, until, when he died in 1946, he weighed less than 100 pounds.

Nobody ever had an unkind word to say about Walter Johnson, off the playing field or on it. And as for the so many tributes to his greatness, one of the choicest was given by the immortal Ty Cobb, one of the greatest hitters and all-around competitors of all time.

Asked what his most embarrassing baseball experience had been, Cobb replied: "Washington on any afternoon with Walter Johnson pitching."

Wide World photos

Christy Mathewson

Christy Mathewson

Christy (for Christopher) Mathewson could quite properly be called the first matinee idol of baseball. He was cut from a far different stripe than most baseball players who fought on the rough-hewn diamonds at the turn of the century. He was a college graduate, tall, handsome and gentle-mannered, a blond, blue-eyed All-American athlete.

Throughout his long and illustrious career with the New York Giants, Christy Mathewson, called Big Six because of his height, never played a baseball game on Sunday.

The grandson of a Civil War hero, Matty, as he was popularly called, was born in 1880 in Factoryville, Pennsylvania. He was one of those boys seemingly blessed with natural grace and the physical attributes to be a great athlete. He began pitching as a lad of thirteen attending Keystone Academy. Then, going on to Bucknell University, at Lewisburg, Pennsylvania, he became a star football player as well as captain of the baseball team. Matty was a true Big Wheel on the campus. He was tremendously popular with his classmates and with the Bucknell faculty, especially since neither vanity nor conceit clouded his pleasant manner.

Matty didn't think about a baseball career during his college days. Salaries weren't very attractive then. But he was a bit at loose ends. He did love sports, and when he was offered eighty dollars a month by Taunton, Massachusetts, of the New England League, he accepted the offer upon graduation from Bucknell.

He didn't show much promise at Taunton, but the

following year, playing for Norfolk, Virginia, he developed a style and pinpoint control. He was winning consistently when Andrew Freedman, owner of the New York Giants, bought his contract and brought him up to the big leagues.

Matty wasn't ready. He lost three straight for Freedman, who promptly shipped him back to Norfolk. There Matty finished out the season, winding up with a tremendous 21-2 record.

Freedman brought him back in 1901. Now, with a full season of Virginia League ball behind him and a taste of the big leagues as well, Matty was ready. He won eight straight games, four of them shutouts. When he was finally stopped by the Cardinals, it was a 1-0 loss.

The Giants were a sorry lot that year. They didn't draw too many fans. Thus, when Matty proved to be such a sensation, and the crowds came out to see him pitch, manager Horace Fogel worked him as often as possible. Anxious to please, Matty tried too hard. He developed a sore arm. From an 8-1 start he went on to a 20-17 finish.

Many of his losses were low-run games, however. The Giants didn't hit behind him. As evidence, Matty compiled a sparkling 1.99 earned-run average that season, and pitched a no-hitter against the Cardinals. But the Giants could do no better than seventh.

The early part of the 1902 season was one of the most dismal in Giants' history. Quickly they settled into last place. Fogel, who seemed vaguely to share the managerial duties with George Smith, thought he might stimulate something by trying Matty out at various other positions. The way the Giants were hitting and fielding, Matty wasn't winning much, anyway.

Fogel tried him at first, then at shortstop. Even in

the outfield. As was his good-natured way, Matty uttered not a complaint. Happily for the fortunes of the Giants and of Matty, the great John McGraw was induced to leave Baltimore and come over to the Giants in the summer of 1902.

McGraw, the fiery "Little Napoleon" who played third base and managed his ball teams with the ferocity of a wounded tiger, quickly restored some semblance of sanity to the Giants.

The first thing he did was restore Matty to the pitcher's mound. Then he got rid of ten ballplayers—including Fogel. He wanted to get rid of Smith, too, when he learned that Smith had agreed with Fogel's opinion that Matty wasn't much of a pitcher. But he needed a second baseman, and Smith was it. So he stayed.

Then McGraw began to raid other teams for talent. He couldn't save the Giants from a last-place finish, or Matty from a terrible 13–18 season, but by the time spring training rolled around in 1903, he had the makings of a great ball team.

McGraw ran a tight ship. He prided himself on well-trained, well-disciplined teams that fought to the final out. He himself was tough as nails, but he had a way of inspiring his men to play their hearts out for him. His intense desire to win was infectious.

This, of course, was the sort of "college spirit" Matty knew. He could respect this. On the other hand, McGraw recognized and respected the soft-spoken good looks of his college-boy pitcher. Though as unlike in background and manner as any two men could be, Matty and McGraw, and later their wives as well, became inseparable friends.

Matty liked to win. What pitcher, what athlete doesn't? But, for McGraw, he wanted to win even more. And he could see around him, in the attitude of his many

new teammates, a reflection of the winning spirit in the 1903 Giants.
In spring training he worked hard at polishing his already fine control. In addition, he developed what he called a "fadeaway pitch." Today it's called a screwball—and Matty was the developer of the pitch.
Aside from Matty, McGraw had "Dummy" Taylor (a deaf mute) and "Iron Man" McGinnity for the nucleus of his pitching staff, and Roger Bresnahan behind the plate—one of the best in the business. A few more shrewd trades early in 1903, and the Giants were ready to roll.
Matty proved to be superb that season. With his new "fadeaway" pitch and excellent control, he won 30 games and lost 13, set what was then a league record of 267 strikeouts while walking 100.
One of Matty's most important assets was his ability to learn. It was more than just the big league pitcher's accumulation of a "book" on the hitters. Matty learned about himself, what he could do well, and where he had flaws.
Remembering well the sore arm that caught up with him two seasons earlier from overwork, he adopted a style of pitching that gave him the maximum efficiency with the minimum of effort. Despite his strikeout record in 1903, he never considered himself a strikeout pitcher. Conversely, his strategy was to let the batter hit the ball, giving him a pitch that would tempt him, but one that would give him just a piece of the ball to hit.
Because of this, his games were shorter than most. He threw many less pitches than the ordinary pitcher threw. The league's batters were well aware of Matty's strategy, but there was nothing to be done about it. They were forced to hit *his* pitch, because it was in the strike zone. Modern pitchers all strive for this effect; it is one of

the first things a manager and a pitching coach will tell a young hurler—try to force the batter to hit *your* pitch. Nobody could do this better than Matty.

Years later Joe Tinker, the famous Cubs' third baseman of Tinker-to-Evers-to-Chance legend, said of Matty: "He wouldn't fool around with you. Other pitchers would throw seven or eight pitches, waste a couple if they could. Not Matty. He'd get rid of you with the first pitch if he could. He hardly ever went three-and-oh or three-and-one on a batter."

This was particularly true after the 1903 season, when, with a full schedule of "fadeaway" pitching behind him, he mastered control of the difficult pitch. Never again did Matty give up as many as 100 walks. Some years his record was incredible. For example, in 1906, while winning 22 games and pitching 267 innings, he walked only 17 men! And in 1913, winning 25 and pitching 306 innings, he walked just 21! That year he set a major league record by pitching 68 consecutive innings without giving up a walk.

The Giants didn't quite make it to the flag in 1903; the Pirates beat them out. Still, McGraw had taken them from last to second place in one season, and in just one more year he took them all the way to the pennant.

Matty was 33–12 in 1904 and 31–9 in 1905, including a 1–0 no-hitter. That gave him three consecutive 30-plus seasons, a major league record.

Matty was such a fantastically consistent winner (for 12 straight years he won more than 20) it's difficult to pick his best year, or even his most outstanding performance. However, he himself always pointed to his feat in the 1905 World Series as his greatest performance. Certainly it was one of the most amazing exhibitions of pitching in a World Series, comparable to Don Larsen's perfect game in 1956 in that Matty's feat was spread over the entire Series.

The 1905 Series pitted McGraw's Giants against Connie Mack's Athletics, a hard-hitting aggregation indeed.

Matty started the first game against Eddie Plank, a 26-game winner for Philadelphia. Plank, a left-hander, was very good. But Matty was better. He blanked the A's, while the Giants got three runs off Plank. Matty didn't walk a man, giving up three singles and a double.

The A's evened the count next day, by the same score. But Matty came back in the third game with another four-hit shutout, winning 9–0.

McGinnity pitched a 1–0 victory in the fourth game. Then, with only one day's rest, Matty came on in the fifth game and pitched his third straight World Series shutout, a 2–0 six-hitter.

Matty's shutout performance has never been equaled in a World Series. (The scoreless strings set later by Babe Ruth, then Whitey Ford, were over a period of several seasons.)

In his 27 shutout innings, Matty fanned 18, while walking but one. He gave up a total of 14 hits, 3 of them doubles, the rest singles.

Because it was a World Series, the feat gave Matty a more satisfying thrill than either of his two no-hitters, and though, three years later, he set a modern major league record by winning 37 games, his World Series of 1905 remained his personal favorite.

That year of 1908, in which he won 37 games, provided one of the classic boners of baseball history. It was one in which Matty was involved, costing him a victory and the Giants the pennant.

It happened on September 22, in the ninth inning of a game against the Cubs.

Matty and Cub pitcher Jack Pfeister were tied up in a 1–1 contest. But now, in the bottom of the ninth, with two out, the Giants had Moose McCormick on third and Fred Merkle on first. Al Bridwell then singled, and McCormick raced home with the winning run.

Only it wasn't the winning run, after all! Apparently with the base hit Merkle had started for second, then, seeing that McCormick would score, simply turned around and headed for the clubhouse.

All was confusion after that. In the excitement, with the overflow crowd swarming onto the field, several versions of what happened next are still in existence. In any case, however, what definitely occurred was that the alert Cub infield yelled for the ball and touched second, claiming a force out and nullifying the tally.

Of course, the Giants screamed it wasn't so. Iron Man McGinnity, in fact, claimed he had taken the ball from Joe Tinker and thrown it into the crowd, and if indeed a force play had been attempted, it was with a new and illegal ball.

Nobody was more confused than the umpires themselves.

The argument raged throughout the afternoon. The Giants left the ball park believing they had won, 2–1. The Cubs claimed it was a tie, or that they should be awarded a 9–0 forfeit because the home team Giants allowed the fans to interfere with the continuance of the game after Merkle was forced at second.

Not until ten o'clock that night did the umpires get together and announce their final decision: The game was a tie and would have to be replayed.

A week later, the season ended in a deadlock between the Giants and Cubs. Without the Merkle boner, the Giants would have won. Matty would have had 38 victories, and been the pennant hero. As it turned out, he pitched in the playoff game between the two clubs and became the goat when he was beaten, 4–2.

The Giants didn't win another pennant until 1911—then they took three straight. Matty was still winning 20-plus season after season. Those were the years, too, when he teamed up with catcher Chief Meyers to form one of the greatest batteries in baseball history. It was the Chief who phrased a description of Matty that was to stand forever as a testimony to the pitcher's fantastic control.

"Anybody can catch Matty," he said. "You could catch him sitting in a rocking chair."

When Matty's career declined, the end came sharply. From a 24–13 record in 1914, he went to 8–14 in 1915. He was thirty-five years old then, and the great arm had exhausted itself.

In July, the following year, when he was 3–4, he went to the Cincinnati Reds as a playing manager. McGraw arranged the deal.

He knew Matty was finished as a pitcher, and he knew, too, that his friend wanted to stay in baseball as a manager. At the same time, McGraw needed infield help, and had his eyes on Whitey Herzog, playing manager for the Reds. Furthermore, he knew Cincinnati owner Garry Herrmann was not satisfied with Herzog.

Accordingly, he approached Herrmann and offered him a trade that would include a Matty-Herzog swap. Herrmann agreed.

Matty knew this was a good thing for him, knew that his pitching days were done. He did hurl one more game—he wanted one in his Cincinnati uniform. He won it, then hung up his glove. Managing the Reds was no bargain for anybody, however. They finished seventh, exactly as they had the season before.

The United States entered World War I in 1917— and Matty gave up baseball for the more important task of winning the war. He was one of the first enlistees. With his college training, he was made an officer, becoming a captain in the Chemical Warfare Division.

It was his job, during the terrible trench fighting, to inspect the American positions to make certain they were not contaminated by poison gas. In the process, he himself was gassed. His lungs were permanently damaged.

He was sent to the hospital at Saranac Lake, New York, to recuperate. Though still weak, he could not resist the call from baseball when it came. In 1923 he was offered the presidency and part ownership of the Boston National League club. Against the advice of his wife and his doctors, Matty took the job.

He worked hard, traveling the country, seeking out promising young players, arranging trades, building up the weak Boston club. The effort sapped the last of his remaining strength.

He was forced back into the hospital in 1925. And there, in October, he died. He was just forty-five years old.

In 1936, Matty was elected to the Hall of Fame.

Below his bronze likeness in the Hall at Cooperstown is an inscription detailing a few of his accomplishments. And below that it says:

"Matty Was the Master of Them All."

Wide World photos

Cy Young

Cy Young ●●●●●●●●●●●●●●●●●●●●●●●●●●●●●●●●

The status of a superstar can often be measured by the fact that baseball fans everywhere recognize his identity by the use of his nickname or by the sole use of his given name. Thus, modern fans, reading the sports page headlines, at once identify Mickey, Willie, Yogi, Whitey or Sandy, for example.

Going back a bit in history, Leo Durocher was universally known as "Lippy," Stan Musial as "The Man," George Herman Ruth as "Babe," Mathewson as "Matty" and Grover Cleveland Alexander as "Ol' Pete" or simply "Alex."

And Denton True Young was Cy.

The Cy was short for Cyclone, the name pinned on Denton by a Canton sportswriter the moment the fireballing right-hander won his professional debut. The name stuck so tightly hardly anybody but his immediate family ever called him anything but Cy after that.

Somehow, the name Cy seemed to fit Denton Young, to suit the big, rawboned farm boy from Gilmore, Ohio. He was a quiet, gentle, serious lad, strong as an ox, a champion rail splitter in the manner of Abraham Lincoln, who died just two years before Denton True Young was born.

That's how far back Cy Young goes. He was born on a farm in 1867, in what used to be Tuscarawa Indian country. Yet his career, certainly the most amazing one in the annals of baseball, went on until 1911. When Cy Young was forty-four years old he was still winning games for the Boston Braves!

Moreover, his career was one that spanned historical decades in baseball. He first pitched from 50 feet away from the plate (instead of the modern 60) and to a catcher who, like himself, wore no glove!

He pitched when there was no American League, and, in fact, helped get the junior league started by joining the Boston Red Sox and adding his great stature to the new league.

And when Cy Young finally retired, he had to his credit 511 victories, a major league record so incredible that there is little doubt it will never be approached, much less bettered. Walter Johnson's 416 victories comes the closest to Cy's record. In modern times only the amazing Warren Spahn has managed to better 350 wins in a lifetime.

When Cy began playing baseball there were no Little Leagues and American Legion teams and supermarkets to sponsor a bunch of youngsters on the sandlots. Amateur baseball, if it could be called that at all, usually meant two teams getting together playing for a small pot of money either gathered from the few spectators or anted by the players themselves.

If a boy was good enough, he might get to play for a town team, backed by a local promoter or businessman, and thus earn a few extra dollars.

That's what Cy was doing, in the spring of 1890, when word got around to the professionals in nearby Canton that there was a pitcher out at Gilmore who could throw a baseball through a brick wall.

Well, Canton manager George Moreland knew Ohio farmers. They could spin more yarns than a gypsy, and telling tall tales was a hobby of theirs. Either they knew a cow that gave twenty quarts of milk a day, or a chicken that laid eggs big as cannonballs or they remembered a hailstorm with stones big as chicken eggs.

And, if they happened to be farmers or traveling salesmen or just in town to buy some feed, and knew a bit about the new game of baseball, they invariably told about some "pheeenomenal" pitcher who threw the ball through a brick wall, or a slugger who hit the ball three counties—and right into the teeth of a cyclone, too.

Still, skeptic though he was, Moreland's interest was piqued by the consistent reports about this pitcher named Denton Young. He took the fifty-mile trip to Gilmore one day, to see for himself. What he saw convinced him at once that here was a spectacular pitcher. Denton Young, as might be expected under the circumstances, had no curve, no fancy tricks. He just threw, in easy rhythm, the fastest baseball Moreland ever saw.

Cy was twenty-three years old then, but family ties were strong on the farm. In the days before radio and television, even before the automobile and electricity, farm families were by nature and necessity closely knit units. When George Moreland offered Cy a job pitching for his Ohio-Pennsylvania League team, therefore, the negotiations also involved the young man's parents.

Moreland offered forty dollars a month as salary. That was four times what Cy earned on the farm. But it was the feeling of the elder Youngs that their boy belonged with them. Playing baseball was all right as long as it was restricted to Tuscarawa County. But leaving home to live in Canton and travel all about the country— well now, that was something else again. Professional baseball players, and baseball in general, did not enjoy the best of reputations around the turn of the century. Particularly in the rural areas, professional athletes were considered somewhat on the level of pool hall gamblers and shady sporting types who frequented race tracks.

To Cy, Moreland seemed to offer an open gateway to adventure. Disappointed by his parents' refusal, he began a campaign of persuasion. He counted heavily on the fact that forty dollars a month wages was quite respectable, even if the profession was questionable. And that was only the beginning. Who could predict how much he might make later on?

Two solid weeks of such arguments finally wore down McKenzie Young and his wife. They sent their boy off to Canton in his one good suit and a cardboard suitcase. When he arrived in the clubhouse of the Canton team he looked indeed the part of the comic "rube," the straw-in-his-hair farm boy trying his luck in the big city.

Cy presented a funny sight—until he pitched. Nobody had seen anything like such blazing speed. Moreland threw him right into action, and before his first victory was tucked away, Denton Young had been tagged "Cyclone" by one of the Canton sportswriters.

Cy was fast all right. But he had no curve and he had no finesse. He just overpowered the hitters. A pitcher can't get away with just that, even in the minor leagues, and even in 1890. Especially when he's pitching for a team that doesn't back him up with runs. Such a team was Canton. Cy won 15 and lost 15 for Canton, a fine record for a young man fresh off the penny-ante sandlots.

There was just one major league in those years, the National, and not much between that and teams like Canton. If a baseball player seemed to have the potential, he could rise to the big league like a shot. Likewise, of course, his fall could be as meteoric.

The year Cy broke in with Canton, the Chicago Colts

were in the process of reorganization under Adrian Anson, known as "Cap." This legendary figure was playing baseball back in 1870 and, with obvious good reason, fancied himself the best judge of talent in the game. But when he came down from Chicago to have a look at Canton's promising new pitcher, he dismissed him with a shrug.

"Young?" he laughed. "Another of them big farmers."

Not everybody in the league took Cap's word for it. Other teams sent scouts around for a look. One of these, Davis Hawley, part owner of the Cleveland Spiders (as they were then known), liked what he saw in young Cy. Further, he knew manager Patsy Lebeau was in desperate need of pitching help. And, finally, Cleveland and Chicago were bitter rivals. It would suit Hawley just fine to beat Anson with a pitcher the Colts' skipper had disdained.

Hawley bought out Cy's contract with Canton before the 1890 season was through and put him to work immediately—against the Colts. Of course, he made certain before the game to advise Cy of Cap Anson's opinion of him.

Cy needed no more inspiration. Any nervousness he might have felt at being thrust so suddenly into big league baseball vanished at the image of Anson's laughingly calling him a "big farmer."

He not only beat the Colts 8–1 that day, he struck out Anson on three straight fast balls the first time they faced each other. Lebeau and Hawley loved him for that performance. Cy worked regularly thereafter—and he was a glutton for work. From the beginning, and throughout his twenty-two years in the major leagues until near the very end, his routine was two days' rest between starts. An occasional relief job came his way, too, on his "rest days," and he sailed into those as though he hadn't pitched in a week.

He won 9 and lost 7 for the Spiders in the latter part of 1890, giving him a total of 24 wins and 22 losses in his first season of professional baseball. Such figures indicate the amount of pitching Cy produced. Exactly how amazing such performances were are further indicated by the fact that he won more than 20 games for 14 straight seasons, beginning with 1891, five times winning more than 30. Yet he never lost less than 10 games a season, and twice in that stretch he was a 20-game loser as well!

With only one league in existence, there was, of course, no World Series. However, in 1894, a Pittsburgh sportsman named William Temple donated a trophy known as the Temple Cup to be awarded the winner of a postseason series between the National League winner and the runner-up: a four-out-of-seven series it was even then, setting the style for the World Series later.

The Spiders qualified in 1895, coming in second behind the famous Baltimore Orioles, the team that boasted such baseball immortals as John McGraw and Willie "Hit 'Em Where They Ain't" Keeler. Cy boasted a 35–10 pitching record.

He beat the powerful Orioles three times in the Cup competition, winning the trophy for Cleveland.

While Cy continued on his splendid way, pitching his first no-hitter in 1897, against Cincinnati, the Spiders' fortunes dwindled. Frank Robison, another part owner of the team, began to look elsewhere for success. At the close of the 1898 season he took over the St. Louis franchise, and with Cy Young as his number-one choice, he moved the best of the Cleveland players to St. Louis.

Cy didn't like the city. Though he won 26 games

there in 1899, and 20 the year after, he wanted out. The oppressive heat of the St. Louis summers sapped his energies (a complaint echoed even today by ball players). He was thirty-three, and he felt that to continue on in St. Louis would shorten his career.

There were many, in fact, who were ready to count him finished. Premature graying and the development of a pot belly added to the evidence of the calendar.

It may well have turned out that continuance in St. Louis would have cut short his playing life. Fortunately, that winter of 1900, a man named Ban Johnson founded the new American League and began raiding the National for talent. To help upgrade the image of his new league he needed players of the highest caliber— famous names who would draw the crowds and give the American League the stature of a true professional organization—a problem encountered several generations later by the upstart American Football League.

One of the first men Johnson approached was Cy Young. He offered Cy $3,000 a year to pitch for the new Boston Red Sox—a $500 increase over his salary with St. Louis. It's likely that the opportunity to move was more tempting than the raise. Cy accepted.

There was intense rivalry between the two leagues, as might be expected. But in 1903 they got together and arranged the first World Series, which was to be a best five-out-of-nine tournament. (It became a seven-game series in 1905.) The Pittsburgh Pirates, with their third straight pennant, represented the National League; the Boston Red Sox, the American.

The first World Series was more than just a clash between pennant winners—it was a test of the American League, which was considered by many baseball observers to be inferior to the National. (Again, the comparison with the status of the American Football League many years later is an apt one. Not until the New York Jets beat the Baltimore Colts in the Super Bowl in 1968 did the AFL gain equality of status.)

Cy dropped the first contest to the Pirates, who won three of the first four games and appeared ready to justify the National League's claim. But Cy came back with two victories in the next three games, and Bill Dinneen won two more, to give the Red Sox and the American League the first World's Championship.

The feeling rampant a few years earlier that Cy Young was just about through changed in Boston to one of wonder if he would *ever* quit. He had won 33 games for the Red Sox in his first year, 32 in 1902, and in the year they beat the Pirates he won 28. Again in 1904 he led Boston to the pennant with a 26–16 record, stopping on the way that season to etch his name even more indelibly in the record books.

On May 5, 1904, Cy went against the hard-hitting Philadelphia Athletics and pitcher Rube Waddell. Cy was thirty-seven years old now; Waddell was ten years younger. The Athletics, too, had such stalwart sluggers on their team as Harry Davis, Socks Seybold, Lave Cross and Danny Murphy.

Twenty-seven Athletics came up, and twenty-seven went down without a man reaching base. Cy pitched the first modern perfect game! (Two perfect games were recorded in 1880 when the game was played under different rules.)

There was no World Series in 1904. John McGraw, manager of the pennant-winning Giants, still refused to recognize the American League and wouldn't participate in the Series.

For the next two years Cy's fortunes waned, and

Boston's with him. Seasons of 18–19 and then 13–21 rekindled the notion that Cy was ready to call it a career. And indeed, when the 1907 season began he was forty years old.

But that rubber arm still had plenty left. In 1907 he amazed the baseball world with a tremendous comeback, winning 22 while losing 15. He was pitching for a second-division ball club now, yet again in 1908 he was a big winner, with a 21–11 record.

What's more, in 1908 he pitched the third no-hitter of his amazing career—at forty-one years of age!

Despite this manifestation of agelessness, the Red Sox believed he was ready for retirement, and traded him to Cleveland, where it had all begun twenty years before.

In truth, Cy was tired, he was terribly fat around the middle, and was about ready to call it quits himself. But the trade to Cleveland brought out the competitive spirit within him. He wanted to prove to the Red Sox that they had been premature in giving up on him, and to reward Cleveland for its faith.

Accordingly, with a supreme effort of will, he turned in a 19–15 season with the Spiders (they weren't called the Indians until 1915), including a two-hit shutout victory over his old Red Sox teammates.

That was just about it for old Cy. He lingered on with the Spiders through 1910 (7–10) and was 3–4 with them in 1911 when they released him in August. He signed on with the Boston Braves, in the National League, won 4 while losing 5 over the balance of the 1911 season.

Then Cy Young finally agreed to hang up his spikes.

He was forty-four years old, with 511 victories to his credit, and three no-hitters.

With his wife, Cy retired to his Ohio farm, but he remained an avid baseball fan for the rest of his life—

which, like his baseball career, was rewarding and long.

Cy was elected to the Hall of Fame in 1937. In November of 1955, at the age of eighty-eight, Denton True "Cyclone" Young died.

Back in Tuscarawa County, Ohio, he is still remembered and talked about as Cy. And there is a Cy Young Park to keep his spirit alive there.

Records

EDWARD CHARLES (WHITEY) FORD

Born October 21, 1928 at New York, N.Y.
Threw and batted lefthanded

Height: 5'10"
Weight: 180

Year	Club	League	G.	IP.	W.	L.	Pct.	H.	R.	ER.	SO.	BB.	ERA.
1947—Butler	Mid. Atl.	24	157	13	4	.765	151	86	67	114	58	3.84
1948—Norfolk	Pied.	30	216	16	8	.667	182	83	62	*171	113	2.58
1949—Binghamton	East.	26	168	16	5	.762	118	38	30	*151	54	*1.61
1950—Kansas City	A. A.	12	95	6	3	.667	81	39	34	80	48	3.22
1950—New York	American	20	112	9	1	.900	87	39	35	59	52	2.81
1951-52—New York						(In Military Service)						
1953—New York	American	32	207	18	6	.750	187	77	69	110	110	3.00
1954—New York	American	34	211	16	8	.667	170	72	66	125	101	2.82
1955—New York	American	39	254	*18	7	.720	188	83	74	137	113	2.62
1956—New York	American	31	226	19	6	*.760	187	70	62	141	84	*2.47
1957—New York	American	24	129	11	5	.688	114	46	37	84	53	2.58
1958—New York	American	30	219	14	7	.667	174	62	49	145	62	*2.01
1959—New York	American	35	204	16	10	.615	194	82	69	114	89	3.04
1960—New York	American	33	193	12	9	.571	168	76	66	85	65	3.08
1961—New York	American.	39	*283	*25	4	*.862	242	108	101	209	92	3.21
1962—New York	American	38	258	17	8	.680	243	90	83	160	69	2.90
1963—New York	American	38	*269	*24	7	*.774	240	94	82	189	56	2.74
1964—New York	American	39	245	17	6	.739	212	67	58	172	57	2.13
1965—New York	American	37	244	16	13	.552	241	97	88	162	50	3.25
1966—New York	American	22	73	2	5	.286	79	33	20	43	24	2.47
1967—New York	American	7	44	2	4	.333	40	11	8	21	9	1.64
Major League Totals		498	3171	236	106	.690	2766	1107	967	1956	1086	2.74

WORLD'S SERIES RECORD

Year Club	League	G.	IP.	W.	L.	Pct.	H.	R.	ER.	SO.	BB.	ERA.
1950—New York	American	1	8⅔	1	0	1.000	7	2	0	7	1	0.00
1953—New York	American	2	8	0	1	.000	9	4	4	7	2	4.50
1955—New York	American	2	17	2	0	1.000	13	6	4	10	8	2.12
1956—New York	American	2	12	1	1	.500	14	8	7	8	2	5.25
1957—New York	American	2	16	1	1	.500	11	2	2	7	5	1.13
1958—New York	American	3	15⅓	0	1	.000	19	8	7	16	5	4.11
1960—New York	American	2	18	2	0	1.000	11	0	0	8	2	0.00
1961—New York	American	2	14	2	0	1.000	6	0	0	7	1	0.00
1962—New York	American	3	19⅔	1	1	.500	24	9	9	12	4	4.12
1963—New York	American	2	12	0	2	.000	10	7	6	8	3	4.50
1964—New York	American	1	5⅓	0	1	.000	8	5	5	4	1	8.44
World's Series Totals		22	146	10	8	.556	132	51	44	94	34	2.71

Won Cy Young Award, 1961

SANFORD (SANDY) KOUFAX

Born December 30, 1935 — Batted right, threw left

Year	Club	League	G.	IP.	W.	L.	Pct.	SO.	BB.	H.	ERA.
1955—Brooklyn [a]	National	12	42	2	2	.500	30	28	33	3.00
1956—Brooklyn	National	16	59	2	4	.333	30	29	66	4.88
1957—Brooklyn	National	34	104	5	4	.556	122	51	83	3.89
1958—Los Angeles	National	40	159	11	11	.500	131	105	132	4.47
1959—Los Angeles	National	35	153	8	6	.571	173	92	136	4.06
1960—Los Angeles	National	37	175	8	13	.381	197	100	133	3.91
1961—Los Angeles	National	42	256	18	13	.581	269	96	212	3.52
1962—Los Angeles [b]	National	28	184	14	7	.667	216	57	134	2.54
1963—Los Angeles [c-d]	National	40	311	25	5	.833	306	58	214	1.88
1964—Los Angeles [e]	National	29	223	19	5	.792	223	53	154	1.74
1965—Los Angeles [f-g]	National	43	336	26	8	.765	382	71	216	2.04
1966—Los Angeles [h-i]	National	41	323	27	9	.750	317	77	241	1.73
Major League Totals ..... 12 yrs.		397	2325	165	87	.655	2396	817	1754	2.76

178

WORLD'S SERIES RECORD

Year	Club	League	G.	IP.	W.	L.	Pct.	SO.	BB.	H.	ERA.
1959—Los Angeles	National		2	9	0	1	.000	7	1	5	1.00
1963—Los Angeles	National		2	18	2	0	1.000	23	3	12	1.50
1965—Los Angeles	National		3	24	2	1	.667	29	5	13	0.38
1966—Los Angeles	National		1	6	0	1	.000	2	2	6	1.50
World's Series Totals			8	57	4	3	.571	61	11	36	0.95

a Signed as bonus player, December 14, 1954. On disabled list May 9 to June 8.
b Pitched no-hit, no-run game against New York Mets, June 30, 1962.
c Pitched no-hit, no-run game against the San Francisco Giants, May 11, 1963.
d Winner of the Cy Young Award as pitcher of the year in the majors in 1963. Selected Most Valuable Player in National League in 1963.
e Pitched no-hit, no-run game against Philadelphia Phillies, June 4, 1964.
f Pitched perfect game against Chicago Cubs, September 9, 1965.
g Winner of the Cy Young Award as pitcher of the year in the majors in 1965.
h Winner of the Cy Young Award as pitcher of the year in the majors in 1966.
i Announced retirement on November 18, 1966.

SPAHN, WARREN EDWARD

Born, Buffalo, New York, April 23, 1921
Threw and batted lefthanded

Height, 6 feet.
Weight, 175 pounds.

Year	Club	League	G.	IP.	W.	L.	Pct.	SO.	BB.	H.	ERA.
1940—Bradford		Pony	12	66	5	4	.556	62	24	53	2.73
1941—Evansville		Three-I	28	212	*19	6	*.760	193	90	154	*1.83
1942—Hartford		Eastern	33	248	17	12	.586	141	130	148	1.96
1942—Boston		National	4	16	0	0	.000	7	11	25	5.63
1943-44-45—Boston		National	(In United States Army)								
1946—Boston		National	24	126	8	5	.615	67	36	107	2.93
1947—Boston		National	40	*290	21	10	.677	123	84	245	*2.33
1948—Boston		National	36	257	15	12	.556	114	77	237	3.71
1949—Boston		National	38	*302	*21	14	.600	*151	86	283	3.07
1950—Boston		National	41	293	*21	17	.553	*191	111	248	3.16
1951—Boston		National	39	311	22	14	.611	*164	*109	278	2.98
1952—Boston		National	40	290	14	19	.424	*183	73	263	2.98
1953—Milwaukee		National	35	266	*23	7	.767	148	70	211	*2.10
1954—Milwaukee		National	39	283	21	12	.636	136	86	262	3.15
1955—Milwaukee		National	39	246	17	14	.548	110	65	249	3.26
1956—Milwaukee		National	39	281	20	11	.645	128	52	249	2.79
1957—Milwaukee		National	39	271	*21	11	.656	111	78	241	2.69
1958—Milwaukee		National	38	*290	*22	11	.583	150	76	257	3.07
1959—Milwaukee		National	40	*292	*21	15	*.667	143	70	282	2.96
1960—Milwaukee		National	40	268	*21	10	.677	154	74	254	3.49
1961—Milwaukee		National	38	263	21	13	.618	115	64	236	*3.01
1962—Milwaukee		National	34	269	18	14	.563	118	55	248	3.04
1963—Milwaukee		National	33	260	23	7	.767	102	49	241	2.60
1964—Milwaukee [a]		National	38	174	6	13	.316	78	52	204	5.28
1965—N.Y.–S.F. [b-c]		National	36	198	7	16	.304	90	56	210	4.00
Major League Totals ...... 21 yrs.			750	5246	363	245	.597	2583	1434	4830	3.08

WORLD'S SERIES RECORD

Year	Club	League	G.	IP.	W.	L.	Pct.	SO.	BB.	H.	ERA.
1948—Boston		National	3	12	1	1	.500	12	3	10	3.00
1957—Milwaukee		National	2	15⅓	1	1	.500	2	2	18	4.70
1958—Milwaukee		National	3	28⅔	2	1	.667	18	8	19	1.88
World's Series Totals			8	56	4	3	.571	32	13	47	2.89

Winner of the Cy Young Award in 1957.
[a] Sold to New York Mets, November 23, 1964.
[b] Released by New York Mets, July 19 and signed by San Francisco Giants, July 22, 1965.
[c] Released by San Francisco Giants, October 15, 1965.

DON DRYSDALE

Year—Club	League	G.	IP.	W.	L.	Pct.	H.	R.	ER.	SO.	BB.	ERA.
1954—Bakersfield	California	15	112	8	5	.615	97	54	43	73	58	3.45
1955—Montreal	Internat'l	28	173	11	11	.500	163	78	64	80	68	3.33
1956—Brooklyn	National	25	99	5	5	.500	95	35	29	55	31	2.64
1957—Brooklyn	National	34	221	17	9	.654	197	76	66	148	61	2.69
1958—Los Angeles	National	44	212	12	13	.480	214	107	98	131	72	4.16
1959—Los Angeles	National	44	271	17	13	.567	237	113	104	*242	93	3.45
1960—Los Angeles	National	41	269	15	14	.517	214	93	85	*246	72	2.84
1961—Los Angeles	National	40	244	13	10	.565	236	111	100	182	83	3.69
1962—Los Angeles	National	43	*314	*25	9	.735	272	122	99	*232	78	2.84
1963—Los Angeles	National	42	315	19	17	.528	*287	114	92	251	57	2.63
1964—Los Angeles	National	40	*321	18	16	.529	242	91	78	237	68	2.19
1965—Los Angeles	National	44	308	23	12	.657	*270	113	95	210	66	2.78
1966—Los Angeles	National	40	274	13	16	.448	279	114	104	177	45	3.42
1967—Los Angeles	National	38	282	13	16	.448	269	101	86	196	60	2.74
1968—Los Angeles	National	31	239	14	12	.538	201	68	57	155	56	2.15
Major League Totals		506	3369	204	162	.558	3013	1258	1093	2462	844	2.93

WORLD'S SERIES RECORD

Year—Club	League	G.	IP.	W.	L.	Pct.	H.	R.	ER.	SO.	BB.	ERA.
1956—Brooklyn	National	1	2	0	0	.000	2	2	2	1	1	9.00
1959—Los Angeles	National	1	7	1	0	1.000	11	1	1	5	4	1.29
1963—Los Angeles	National	1	9	1	0	1.000	3	0	0	9	1	0.00
1965—Los Angeles	National	2	11⅔	1	1	.500	12	9	5	15	3	3.86
1966—Los Angeles	National	2	10	0	2	.000	8	5	5	6	3	4.50
World's Series Totals		7	39⅔	3	3	.500	36	17	13	36	12	2.95

ROBERT (HOOT) GIBSON

Born November 9, 1935, at Omaha, Nebraska
Throws Right Bats Right
Height 6'1"
Weight 193

Year	Club	League	G.	IP.	W.	L.	Pct.	H.	R.	ER.	SO.	BB.	ERA.
1957	Omaha	A.A.	10	42	2	1	.667	46	26	20	25	27	4.29
1957	Columbus	Sally	8	43	4	3	.571	36	26	18	24	34	3.77
1958	Omaha	A.A.	13	87	3	4	.429	79	45	32	47	39	3.31
1958	Rochester	Internat'l	20	103	5	5	.500	88	35	28	75	54	2.45
1959	Omaha	A.A.	24	135	9	9	.500	128	59	46	98	70	3.07
1959	St. Louis	National	13	76	3	5	.375	77	35	28	48	39	3.32
1960	St. Louis	National	27	87	3	6	.333	97	61	54	69	48	5.59
1960	Rochester	Internat'l	6	41	2	3	.400	33	15	13	36	17	2.85
1961	St. Louis	National	35	211	13	12	.520	186	91	76	166	*119	3.24
1962	St. Louis	National	32	234	15	13	.536	174	84	74	208	95	2.85
1963	St. Louis	National	36	255	18	9	.667	224	110	96	204	96	3.39
1964	St. Louis	National	40	287	19	12	.613	250	106	96	245	86	3.01
1965	St. Louis	National	38	299	20	12	.625	243	110	102	270	103	3.07
1966	St. Louis	National	35	280	21	12	.636	210	90	76	225	78	2.44
1967	St. Louis	National	24	175	13	7	.650	151	62	58	147	40	2.98
1968	St. Louis	National	34	305	22	9	.710	198	49	38	268	62	1.12
Major League Totals			314	2209	147	97	.603	1810	798	698	1850	766	2.85

WORLD'S SERIES RECORD

Year	Club	League	G.	IP.	W.	L.	Pct.	H.	R.	ER.	SO.	BB.	ERA.
1964	St. Louis	National	3	27	2	1	.667	23	11	9	31	8	3.00
1967	St. Louis	National	3	27	3	0	1.000	14	3	3	26	5	1.00
1968	St. Louis	National	3	27	2	1	.667	18	5	5	35	4	1.67
World's Series Totals			9	81	7	2	.778	55	19	17	92	17	1.89

183

GROVER CLEVELAND (PETE) ALEXANDER

Born, Feb. 26, 1887, at St. Paul, Neb.
Died, Nov. 4, 1950, at St. Paul, Neb.

Height, 6'1". Weight, 185.
Threw and batted righthanded.
Elected to Hall of Fame in 1938

Year	Club	League	G.	IP.	W.	L.	Pct.	H.	R.	ER.	SO.	BB.	ERA.
1909	Galesburg	Ill.-Mo.	24	219	15	8	.652	124	49	...	198	42	...
1910	Syracuse	N. Y. State	*43	245	*29	14	.674	215	...	...	204	67	...
1911	Philadelphia	National	48	*367	*28	13	.683	285	133	97	227	129	2.81
1912	Philadelphia	National	46	†310	19	17	.528	289	133	96	*195	105	2.82
1913	Philadelphia	National	47	306	22	8	.733	288	106	94	159	75	2.39
1914	Philadelphia	National	46	*355	†27	15	.643	*327	133	51	*214	76	*1.22
1915	Philadelphia	National	49	*376	*31	10	*.756	253	86	51	*241	64	*1.22
1916	Philadelphia	National	48	*389	*33	12	.733	*323	90	67	*167	50	*1.55
1917	Philadelphia a	National	45	*388	*30	13	.698	*326	107	79	*200	56	*1.83
1918	Chicago	National	3	26	2	1	.667	19	7	5	15	3	1.78
1919	Chicago	National	30	235	16	11	.593	180	51	45	121	38	*1.72
1920	Chicago	National	46	*363	*27	14	.659	*335	96	77	*173	69	*1.91
1921	Chicago	National	31	252	15	13	.536	286	110	95	77	33	3.39
1922	Chicago	National	33	246	16	13	.552	283	111	99	48	34	3.62
1923	Chicago	National	39	305	22	12	.647	308	128	108	72	30	3.19
1924	Chicago	National	21	169	12	5	.706	183	82	57	33	25	3.03
1925	Chicago	National	32	236	15	11	.577	270	106	89	63	29	3.39
1926	Chi.b-St. Louis	National	30	200	12	10	.545	191	83	68	47	31	3.06
1927	St. Louis	National	37	268	21	10	.677	261	94	75	48	38	2.52
1928	St. Louis	National	34	244	16	9	.640	262	106	91	59	37	3.36
1929	St. Louis c	National	22	132	9	8	.529	149	65	57	33	23	3.89
1930	Philadelphia	National	9	22	0	3	.000	40	24	22	6	6	9.00
1930	Dallas	Texas	5	24	1	2	.333	35	23	22	4	11	8.25
Major League Totals			696	5189	373	208	.642	4868	1851‡	1372	2198	951	‡2.56

WORLD'S SERIES RECORD

Year	Club	League	G.	IP.	W.	L.	Pct.	H.	R.	ER.	SO.	BB.	ERA.
1915—Philadelphia	National	2	17⅔	1	1	.500	14	3	3	10	4	1.58
1926—St. Louis	National	3	20⅓	2	0	1.000	12	4	2	17	4	0.89
1928—St. Louis	National	2	5	0	1	.000	10	11	11	2	4	19.80
World's Series Totals			7	43	3	2	.600	36	18	16	29	12	3.35

‡ Does not include 1911 season when earned runs were not compiled.

ᵃ Traded with Catcher William Killefer to Chicago Cubs for Pitcher Mike Prendergast, Catcher Pickles Dilhoefer and $60,000, November 11, 1917.

ᵇ Waived to St. Louis Cardinals, June 22, 1926.

ᶜ Traded to Philadelphia Phillies with Catcher Harry McCurdy for Outfielder Homer Peel and Pitcher Bob McGraw, December 11, 1929.

DENNIS DALE McLAIN

Born March 29, 1944, Chicago, Illinois
Bats Right Throws Right

Height 6'1"
Weight 186

Year	Club	League	G.	IP.	W.	L.	Pct.	H.	R.	ER.	SO.	BB.	ERA.
1962—Harlan		Appal.	2	18	1	1	.500	9	2	0	32	10	0.00
1962—Clinton		Midwest	16	91	4	7	.364	92	54	36	93	37	3.56
1963—Duluth-Superior		Northern	18	141	13	2	*.867	117	47	40	157	51	2.55
1963—Knoxville		Sally	11	77	5	4	.556	61	34	30	82	28	3.51
1963—Detroit		American	3	21	2	1	.667	20	12	10	22	16	4.29
1964—Syracuse		Internat'l	8	59	3	1	.750	38	13	10	56	18	1.53
1964—Detroit		American	19	100	4	5	.444	84	48	45	70	37	4.05
1965—Detroit		American	33	220	16	6	.727	174	73	64	192	62	2.62
1966—Detroit		American	38	264	20	14	.588	205	*120	*115	192	104	3.92
1967—Detroit		American	37	235	17	16	.515	209	110	99	161	73	3.79
1968—Detroit		American	41	336	31	6	.838	241	86	73	280	63	1.96
Major League Totals			171	1176	90	48	.655	933	449	406	917	355	3.10

WORLD'S SERIES RECORD

Year	Club	League	G.	IP.	W.	L.	Pct.	H.	R.	ER.	SO.	BB.	ERA.
1968—Detroit		American	3	16⅔	1	2	.333	18	8	6	13	4	3.24

WALTER PERRY (BARNEY) JOHNSON

Born Nov. 6, 1887, Humboldt, Kansas.
Died Dec. 10, 1946, Washington, D.C.

Threw and batted righthanded
Elected to Hall of Fame in 1936

Year	Club	League	G.	IP.	W.	L.	Pct.	ShO.	H.	R.	ER.	SO.	BB.	ERA.
1907—Washington	American	14	111	5	9	.357	2	100	35		70	16	
1908—Washington	American	36	257	14	14	.500	6	196	75		160	52	
1909—Washington	American	40	297	13	25	.342	4	247	112		164	84	
1910—Washington	American	†45	*374	25	17	.595	8	*262	92		*313	76	
1911—Washington	American	40	322	25	13	.658	6	292	117		207	70	
1912—Washington	American	50	368	32	12	.727	7	259	89		*303	76	
1913—Washington	American	48	*346	*36	7	*.837	*12	232	56	44	*243	38	*1.14
1914—Washington	American	*51	*372	*28	18	.609	*10	*287	88	71	*225	74	1.72
1915—Washington	American	47	*337	*27	13	.675	†8	258	83	58	*203	56	1.55
1916—Washington	American	48	*371	*25	20	.556	3	*290	105	78	*228	82	1.89
1917—Washington	American	47	328	23	16	.590	8	259	105	83	*188	67	2.28
1918—Washington	American	39	325	*23	13	.639	†8	241	71	46	*162	70	*1.27
1919—Washington	American	39	290	20	14	.588	*7	235	73	48	*147	51	*1.49
1920—Washington	American	21	144	8	10	.444	4	135	68	50	78	27	3.13
1921—Washington	American	35	264	17	14	.548	1	265	122	103	*143	92	3.51
1922—Washington	American	41	280	15	16	.484	*4	283	115	93	105	99	2.99
1923—Washington	American	42	261	17	12	.586	3	263	114	101	*130	69	3.48
1924—Washington	American	38	278	*23	7	*.767	*6	233	97	84	*158	77	*2.72
1925—Washington	American	30	229	20	7	.741	3	211	95	78	108	78	3.07
1926—Washington	American	33	262	15	16	.484	2	259	120	105	125	73	3.61
1927—Washington	American	18	108	5	6	.455	1	113	70	61	48	26	5.08
1928—Newark	Internat'l	1	0	0	0	.000	0	0	0	0	0	1	0.00
Major League Totals		802	5924	416	270	.599	113	4920	1902		3508	1353	

WORLD'S SERIES RECORD

Year	Club	League	G.	IP.	W.	L.	Pct.	ShO.	H.	R.	ER.	SO.	BB.	ERA.
1924—Washington	American	3	24	1	2	.333	0	30	10	9	20	11	3.38
1925—Washington	American	3	26	2	1	.667	1	26	10	6	15	4	2.08
World's Series Totals		6	50	3	3	.500	1	56	20	15	35	15	2.70

CHRISTOPHER (BIG SIX) MATHEWSON

Born Aug. 12, 1880, Factoryville, Pa.
Died Oct. 7, 1925, Saranac Lake, N.Y.
Batted and threw righthanded

Height 6'1"
Weight 195
Elected to Hall of Fame in 1936

Year	Club	League	G.	IP.	W.	L.	Pct.	ShO.	H.	R.	ER.	SO.	BB.	ERA.
1899	Taunton	N. Eng.	17	...	5	2	.714	...	...	...	...	...	...	...
1900	Norfolk	Virginia	22	187	20	2	.909	4	119	59	...	128	27	...
1900	New York [a]	Virginia	22	187	20	2	*.909	4	119	59	...	128	27	...
1901	New York	National	6	34	0	3	.000	0	34	32	...	15	20	...
1902	New York	National	34	276	14	17	.452	8	241	114	...	162	74	...
1903	New York	National	45	367	30	13	.698	3	320	136	...	*267	100	...
1904	New York	National	48	368	33	12	.783	4	306	120	...	*212	78	...
1905	New York	National	43	339	*31	9	.775	*9	252	85	...	*206	64	...
1906	New York	National	38	267	22	12	.647	7	262	100	...	128	17	...
1907	New York	National	41	315	*24	12	.667	9	250	88	...	*178	53	...
1908	New York	National	*56	391	*37	11	.771	*12	281	85	...	*259	42	...
1909	New York	National	37	274	25	6	†.806	8	192	57	...	149	36	...
1910	New York	National	38	319	*27	9	.750	2	291	98	...	*190	57	...
1911	New York	National	45	307	26	13	.667	5	*303	102	...	141	38	...
1912	New York	National	43	†310	23	12	.657	0	311	107	73	134	34	2.12
1913	New York	National	40	306	25	11	.694	5	†291	93	70	93	21	*2.06
1914	New York	National	41	312	24	13	.648	5	314	133	*104	80	23	3.00
1915	New York	National	27	186	8	14	.364	1	199	97	74	57	20	3.58
1916	N.Y.[b]	Cinn.	National	13	74	4	4	.500	1	74	35	25	19	8	3.04
Major League Totals			635	4781	373	188	.665	83	4203	1613	...	2505	837	...

WORLD'S SERIES RECORD

Year	Club	League	G.	IP.	W.	L.	Pct.	ShO.	H.	R.	ER.	SO.	BB.	ERA.
1905—New York	National		3	27	3	0	1.000	3	14	0	0	18	1	0.00
1911—New York	National		3	27	1	2	.333	0	25	8	7	13	2	2.33
1912—New York	National		3	28⅔	0	2	.000	0	23	11	5	10	5	1.57
1913—New York	National		2	19	1	1	.500	1	14	3	1	7	2	0.47
World's Series Totals			11	101⅔	5	5	.500	4	76	22	13	48	10	1.15

[a] Joined Giants mid-season, 1900. Turned back to Norfolk at end of campaign, but drafted by Cincinnati and traded to Giants for Pitcher Amos Rusie.
[b] Traded with Outfielder Edd Roush to Cincinnati for Infielder Charles Herzog and Outfielder Wade Killefer, July 20, 1916.

DENTON TRUE (CY) YOUNG

Born, March 29, 1867, at Gilmore, O.
Died, November 4, 1955, at Peoli, O.

Height, 6'2". Weight, 210
Threw and batted righthanded.

Elected to Hall of Fame in 1937.

Year	Club	League	G.	IP.	W.	L.	Pct.	ShO.	H.	R.	SO.	BB.
1890	Canton	Tri-State	31	260	15	15	.500	0	253	165	201	33
1890	Cleveland	National	17	150	9	7	.563	0	145	83	36	32
1891	Cleveland	National	54	430	27	20	.574	0	436	239	146	132
1892	Cleveland	National	53	455	36	11	*.766	9	362	159	167	114
1893	Cleveland	National	53	426	32	16	.667	1	441	229	102	104
1894	Cleveland	National	52	409	25	22	.532	2	493	266	101	101
1895	Cleveland	National	47	373	*35	10	.778	4	371	176	120	77
1896	Cleveland	National	51	414	29	16	.644	5	467	212	137	64
1897	Cleveland	National	47	338	21	18	.538	2	389	195	87	50
1898	Cleveland a	National	46	378	25	14	.641	1	394	174	107	40
1899	St. Louis	National	44	369	26	15	.634	4	364	170	112	43
1900	St. Louis	National	41	321	20	18	.526	4	337	146	119	38
1901	Boston	American	43	371	*33	10	.767	5	320	113	*159	38
1902	Boston	American	45	386	*32	10	.762	3	337	137	166	51
1903	Boston	American	40	342	*28	10	.737	7	292	116	183	37
1904	Boston	American	43	380	26	16	.619	10	326	104	203	28
1905	Boston	American	38	321	18	19	.486	5	245	98	208	30
1906	Boston	American	39	288	13	†21	.382	0	289	135	146	27
1907	Boston	American	43	343	22	15	.595	6	287	101	148	52
1908	Boston b	American	36	299	21	11	.656	3	230	68	150	37
1909	Cleveland	American	35	295	19	15	.559	3	267	110	109	59
1910	Cleveland	American	21	163	7	10	.412	1	149	62	58	27
1911	Cleveland c	American	7	46	3	4	.429	0	54	28	20	13
1911	Boston	National	11	80	4	5	.444	2	83	47	35	15
American League Totals			390	3234	222	141	.612	43	2796	1072	1550	399
National League Totals			516	4143	289	172	.627	34	4282	2096	1269	810
Major League Totals			906	7377	511	313	.620	77	7078	3168	2819	1209

TEMPLE CUP RECORD

Year	Club	League	G.	IP.	W.	L.	Pct.	ShO.	H.	R.	SO.	BB.
1895—Cleveland		National	3	27	3	0	1.000	0	27	7	2	4
1896—Cleveland		National	1	9	0	1	.000	0	13	7	0	1
Temple Cup Totals			4	36	3	1	.750	0	40	14	2	5

WORLD SERIES RECORD

Year	Club	League	G.	IP.	W.	L.	Pct.	ShO.	H.	R.	SO.	BB.
1903—Boston		American	4	33	2	1	.667	0	31	13	17	4

[a] Transferred with pick of team to St. Louis by Frank Robison, owner of both clubs.
[b] Sold to Cleveland for $12,500.
[c] Released, August, 1911, and signed with Boston N. L.